The Statue of Liberty

The Statue

Yale UNIVERSITY PRESS

NEW HAVEN & LONDON

of Liberty

A Transatlantic Story

Edward Berenson

Published with assistance from the foundation established in memory of
Philip Hamilton McMillan of the Class of 1894, Yale College.

Yale University Press books may be purchased in quantity for educational,
business, or promotional use. For information, please e-mail sales.press@
yale.edu (U.S. office) or sales@yaleup.co.uk (U.K. office).

Set in Janson type by Integrated Publishing Solutions.
Printed in the United States of America.

Library of Congress Cataloging-in-Publication Data

Berenson, Edward, 1949–
The Statue of Liberty : a transatlantic story / Edward Berenson.
    p.   cm.—(Icons of America)
Includes bibliographical references and index.
ISBN 978-0-300-14950-0 (hardcover : alk. paper)

  1. Statue of Liberty (New York, N.Y.)—History. 2. Bartholdi, Frédéric-
Auguste, 1834–1904. 3. New York (N.Y.)—Buildings, structures, etc.—
History. 4. United States—Relations—France. 5. France—Relations—
United States. I. Title.
    F128.64.L6B47   2012
    974.7′1—dc23   2011049636

A catalogue record for this book is available from the British Library.

10 9 8 7 6 5 4 3 2 1

Icons of America

Mark Crispin Miller, Series Editor

Icons of America is a series of short works written by leading scholars, critics, and writers, each of whom tells a new and innovative story about American history and culture through the lens of a single iconic individual, event, object, or cultural phenomenon.

The Hollywood Sign: Fantasy and Reality of an American Icon, by Leo Braudy

Joe DiMaggio: The Long Vigil, by Jerome Charyn

The Big House: Image and Reality of the American Prison, by Stephen Cox

Andy Warhol, by Arthur C. Danto

Our Hero: Superman on Earth, by Tom De Haven

Fred Astaire, by Joseph Epstein

Wall Street: America's Dream Palace, by Steve Fraser

No Such Thing as Silence: John Cage's 4' 33", by Kyle Gann

Frankly, My Dear: Gone with the Wind *Revisited*, by Molly Haskell

Alger Hiss and the Battle for History, by Susan Jacoby

Nearest Thing to Heaven: The Empire State Building and American Dreams, by Mark Kingwell

Unwarranted Influence: Dwight D. Eisenhower and the Military-Industrial Complex, by James Ledbetter

The Liberty Bell, by Gary Nash

The Hamburger: A History, by Josh Ozersky

Gypsy: The Art of the Tease, by Rachel Shteir

King's Dream, by Eric J. Sundquist

Jackson Pollock, by Evelyn Toynton

Inventing a Nation: Washington, Adams, Jefferson, by Gore Vidal

Bob Dylan: Like a Complete Unknown, by David Yaffe

Small Wonder: The Little Red Schoolhouse in History and Memory, by Jonathan Zimmerman

For Catherine, Pat, and Bob

Contents

Acknowledgments xi

Prologue 1

ONE
The Idea 8

TWO
Paying for It 30

THREE
Building It 57

FOUR
American Reticence? 73

FIVE
The Unveiling 90

Contents

SIX

Huddled Masses   103

SEVEN

From Neglect to Commemoration   126

EIGHT

The Popular Imagination   140

NINE

Restoration   166

TEN

The Centennial Celebration   181

Coda: 2011   194

Notes   199
Index   213

Acknowledgments

I wish to thank the wonderful archivists and librarians at the Conservatoire national des arts et métiers in Paris. They were generous with their time and advice and helped me locate materials I would otherwise have missed. I'm grateful to Ruth Harris, who read and commented on the entire manuscript. I wouldn't think of submitting a manuscript without having her read it first. I'm thankful as well for Gary Nash's careful reading and astute advice about the text. (Any mistakes are, of course, my own.) Finally, I'd like to acknowledge John Palmer and Jeffrey Schier for their fine editorial work; John Rambow, proofreader extraordinaire; and Sandy Dijkstra for everything.

I found several existing works crucial as I prepared my own, and I'd like to acknowledge them here: Barry Moreno, *The Statue of Liberty Encyclopedia* (New York: Simon & Schuster, 2000); Pierre Provoyeur and June Hargrove, *Liberty: The French-American Statue in Art and History* (New York: Harper & Row, 1986); Marvin Trachtenberg, *The Statue of Liberty* (New York: Penguin, 1976); Robert Belot and Daniel Bermond, *Bartholdi* (Paris: Perrin, 2004); and Albert Boime,

Hollow Icons: The Politics of Sculpture in 19th-Century France (Kent, Ohio: Kent State University Press, 1987).

As always, my greatest debt of gratitude is to my wife, Catherine Johnson, whose sharp intelligence and beautiful prose give me inspiration every day.

This book is dedicated to Catherine and to the memory of her parents, Robert Johnson (d. 2010) and Patricia Johnson (d. 2011), whose love, warmth, and generosity we will always miss.

The Statue of Liberty

Prologue

It's a cold March morning, and I'm late for my 9:30 a.m. excursion to the Statue of Liberty. As I sprint toward the dock, hoping I'll make my boat, a solid wall of people stops me short. Hundreds, maybe thousands, of ticket holders are waiting to get onboard. The queue snakes around a maze of metal barriers; its destination is not the ferry but a huge bubble structure like those that cover tennis courts in chilly winter months. My ferry reservation is meaningless; it's the security officers inside who determine when people get on.

"Hats, belt, watches, wallets, coats, shoes. Hats, belts, watches, wallets, coats, shoes," I hear the officers chant as I'm finally admitted to the security bubble's relative warmth. I've spent a solid hour in the cold. About three million people visit Liberty Island every year, and even in winter they're willing to stand patiently, sometimes an entire morning, in the brisk air of Battery Park. Another thirty minutes go by before I'm finally invited to surrender my outerwear and metallic effects to the National Park Service's security routine.

It's hard to imagine a more tempting terrorist target than the Statue of Liberty. To destroy Lady Liberty would be to strike at the symbolic heart of the United States. It's more than painful enough to

I

contemplate a Manhattan skyline rendered toothless by Al Qaeda's assault. Without the Statue of Liberty, New York Harbor would be damaged beyond emotional repair, a historical essence of America erased for good.

It would be a terrible loss not just for us, but also for the French, whose forebears had created the statue as a gift to the United States. One day, not long after 9/11, my then seven-year-old son was abruptly overcome by worry that someone would hit the statue next. What if terrorists fly an airplane into the Statue of Liberty, he asked my wife, his face betraying the fear that she would have no answer to give. As it turned out, he didn't need one. "The French people are so nice," he said, "they would make us a new one."

Inside the security station, I hear a great many French voices. The Statue of Liberty is a de rigueur Manhattan stop for those whose countrymen conceived and constructed the monument nearly a century and a half ago. One middle-aged Frenchman leading a group of school-age kids waxes enthusiastic about the statue's history and the ideals it represents. Americans have much less bureaucracy, he says, and it's amazing that a black man could become president. Like many others from his native country, he loves the idea of America, its allergy to hierarchies of class and inherited status, its optimism and ethic of freedom, and especially the freedom to create oneself.

Listening to these Gallic accents, I'm swept up in their enthusiasm. Like them, I feel the presence of something much greater than myself. I'm awed in a religious sense as I stand on the southern tip of Manhattan looking out at the great green goddess that symbolizes liberty, hospitality, and opportunity—all that's best about America itself.

No image is more widely recognized. Lady Liberty adorns everything from the logo of an insurance company to greeting cards from NARAL Pro-Choice America. But how well do we really know the

Statue of Liberty? How familiar is its history and symbolism, its transplantation from a French sculptor's studio to the shores of New York? How many of us understand its political and cultural trajectory from French academic statuary to icon of American pop? The Statue of Liberty is, in short, a transatlantic phenomenon, a give-and-take between France and the United States, between high culture and popular taste.

Partly for this reason, it has come to symbolize America while also signifying a set of powerful values that people in Europe and elsewhere can embrace. But those values have not remained stable over the years. Ever since its first images appeared in the mid-1870s, even before construction in Paris had begun, the colossus of New York Harbor has been an open figurative screen, a massive sculpted form onto which an endless variety of ideas, values, intentions, and emotions could be projected. One of the statue's most startling qualities has been to change its apparent meaning from one decade or generation to the next and even to represent, all at once, several opposing qualities: liberty and subjection; immigration and xenophobia; the lure of America and its dangerous shoals; a future of hope and a past of despair; and, of course, Franco-American friendship and French-American distaste.

According to the art historian Albert Boime, our extremely fluid understanding of what the statue says comes from three of its essential qualities: abstractness, artistic banality, and colossal size.[1] Its creator, Frédéric Auguste Bartholdi, intended the Statue of Liberty to last many decades, even centuries, and wanted it to express a general, universal theme. He also hoped that the often-dramatic changes inherent in liberal societies wouldn't render it obsolete. He thus gave it a classical form, one that had endured since ancient times, and kept it abstract and allegorical rather having it represent a particular individual or historical event. The Statue of Liberty doesn't even overtly refer to the United States.

True, Bartholdi inscribed the date July 4, 1776, on its tablet, but that inscription is invisible from afar and, in any case, holds meaning for people other than Americans, just like July 14, 1789, or September 11, 2001. And, of course, the meanings of all three dates are themselves highly contested both within the countries directly involved—France and the United States—and elsewhere in the world. Some see Bastille Day as representing liberation from oppression, while others see its violence as prefiguring the Reign of Terror. For virtually all Americans, 9/11 stands as a day of tragedy and unwarranted suffering and death, but some see it as an act of war authored by our political enemies while others consider it purely a crime, if a particularly heinous one. At the same time, an uncomfortable number of people see 9/11 not as a tragedy but as a victory, as the successful punishment of a country believed guilty of oppressing and exploiting the Muslim world. July 4 is less controversial, though those who dislike the United States hardly want to celebrate the nation whose creation it represents.

Like its abstractness, the Statue of Liberty's artistic banality—its conservatism of form—is related to its need to survive political and cultural change. Bartholdi himself admitted that his statue "cannot be considered as a very great work of art."[2] But its neutral neoclassicism allowed it to elude passionate aesthetic attack and gave it the potential to represent a great many different things. Finally, the statue's colossal size and strategic location guaranteed that it would continue to draw attention and thus retain the ability to encourage people to confer meaning on it, whether for political, social, or commercial purposes.

One of the best ways to contemplate both the fluidity and the durability of the Statue of Liberty is to jog or walk along the Hudson River toward Battery Park. I run there often, and every time I round a minipeninsula jutting into the river I'm startled as Liberty comes brilliantly into view. With each step I see her from a slightly different angle, and she changes subtly but perceptibly as I move closer to her, turning west and then south. On each outing, it's as if I'm seeing her for the first time. Though I know she's been planted there in the harbor for more than a century, she seems an apparition, a Venus rising from the sea, just as Bartholdi intended when he chose Bedloe's Island for her site.

Jogging toward the Statue of Liberty is one thing, visiting it quite another. Once we're finally released from security and onto the boat, I climb to the unsheltered upper deck, where it's bitterly, unexpectedly cold. But it would be senseless to watch Liberty approach through the grimy windows below, so I resist going inside. As the ferry inches toward Liberty Island, I gradually perceive just how very big the statue is. Its foundation looks like a medieval fortress, the pedestal a monument in itself. Most surprising is Liberty's color. From a distance she looks sea green, but up close she's a delicate pastel color, the natural green of her oxidized copper. I can see the seams of the three hundred copper sheets Bartholdi hammered into wafers no wider (3/32 of an inch) than a delicate pastry shell.

I haven't been to the Statue of Liberty since the sixth grade. Back then we could readily climb to the top and look out her windowed crown; today, in the wake of 9/11, visitors can go inside only with a special pass, booked months in advance. The lucky few undergo a second security screening, no bags of any kind allowed. We'd learned on the boat that the statue represents, as the recording put it, "freedom, opportunity, security, and the future." Post-9/11, the security is so tight that most visitors must remain outside.

As our ferry docks, another boat comes in from New Jersey's Liberty State Park. My mind flashes on *The Sopranos*' famous credit sequence in which Tony passes by this very park. As his SUV glides down the New Jersey Turnpike, the roadway cutting a wide swath through Liberty International (Newark) Airport, the camera focuses on one Jersey landmark after another, landmarks destined to become as familiar as Tony Soprano's lit cigar. A few seconds into the sequence, we glimpse the Statue of Liberty, but here on the New Jersey side of the harbor we can see her only from behind. She's thin and distant and obscured in a mist of quasi-impressionist trees. Almost never before has a camera depicted Liberty from this backward, hazy point of view. It is a disturbing, unsettling image, one that evokes the shadows behind her back. From this angle Bartholdi's original title, "Liberty Enlightening the World," seems anachronistic at best.

Here on Liberty Island, I want to gaze at the monument from the front. Walking toward it, I encounter a row of bronze statues depicting the five key figures, three French and two American, from the statue's history. The first represents Edouard René de Laboulaye, the French legal scholar and historian of the United States, credited, perhaps falsely, with conceiving the idea of a great, liberty-affirming French gift to the United States. Next comes Bartholdi, the dauntless sculptor fascinated by the colossi of ancient Egypt who decided that only a new colossus could fulfill Laboulaye's dream. Then there's Gustave Eiffel, the visionary engineer who built the statue's elegant skeleton of iron, an incipient Eiffel Tower lurking within Bartholdi's giant neoclassical form.

Together, Laboulaye, Bartholdi, and Eiffel—intellectual, artist, and engineer—transformed the Statue of Liberty from abstract idea to material presence in the world. They represent the grand nineteenth-century French faith that freedom and progress go hand in hand, and that art can advance them both.

The final two bronzes depict the Americans Joseph Pulitzer and Emma Lazarus. The former used his sensationalist New York *World* to raise the individual contributions without which the Statue of Liberty might never have gone up. The latter composed the poem whose stanzas, recited millions of times since she wrote them in 1883, would never go stale. Conceived as an altar of liberty, Bartholdi's statue would come to represent Lazarus's "huddled masses yearning to breathe free."

Approaching the colossal statue's base, I pass a young Frenchwoman posing for a picture with the green lady looming right behind. The tourist raises her right arm, as if holding Liberty's torch, and imitates the statue's form. As I watch her, my mind wanders back to images I'd seen of the French Revolution, when young women dressed themselves as Roman goddesses of liberty, as if living exemplars of the revolutionary motto: liberty, equality, and fraternity. I have no idea what today's Frenchwoman has in mind, but her face is solemn, her pose studied and apparently sincere. It's as if she too has become, however momentarily, a goddess of liberty, a souvenir in her own right of France's gift to the United States.

As I look upward at the great green lady, she appears to step forward. Her robes show movement at the bottom, her knee bends, and her back heel points up off the ground as if in mid-stride. Liberty's face may be serene, but her body moves into the whirlwind of liberty that blew in from across the sea and "made here," as President Grover Cleveland put it, "its home."

ONE

The Idea

This story begins, as many French stories do, around a dinner table. It was early summer of 1865, the locale a charming village just southwest of Paris. The French legal scholar Edouard de Laboulaye had gathered an intimate group of like-minded liberals at his well-appointed country residence in Glatigny. The group included Oscar de Lafayette, grandson of George Washington's comrade in arms; Count Charles de Rémusat, whose wife was another of Lafayette's grandchildren; Hippolyte de Tocqueville, brother of the deceased author of *Democracy in America*; and a young up-and-coming sculptor named Frédéric Auguste Bartholdi, future architect of the Statue of Liberty. By any measure, this was a distinguished circle of men.

Their liberalism must be understood in its nineteenth-century sense. Laboulaye and his guests occupied a sliver of centrist political ground, with conservative Catholics, monarchists, and supporters of Napoleon III, the current ruler, on their right, and progressive republicans, democrats, and socialists on their left. In terms of social standing, Laboulaye and his guests resembled much of the right, but they shared with the left a distaste for Napoleon III's authoritarian government and a desire for the individual liberties he had suppressed.

Laboulaye stood out as France's leading authority on the United States, and although constraints on free speech discouraged him from saying so directly, he preferred the American political system to recent and prevailing ones in France. The Frenchman liked America's strong tradition of individual liberty, the checks and balances that limited the size and reach of government, and its optimistic belief in individual advancement through schooling, civic involvement, and membership in voluntary associations. Laboulaye had published many books, some more polemical than scholarly, and he taught a popular course at the prestigious Collège de France. His best-known work was a three-volume *History of the United States* (1862–66). The professor's polemical writing appeared mainly in the *Journal des Débats*, a politically moderate newspaper in which he gently advocated individual rights vis-à-vis the state. He even published two novels, one of which, *Paris in America* (1864), made fun of French political habits by comparing them to American ones.[1]

The ostensible reason for his dinner party was to celebrate the North's victory in the American Civil War and to mourn the death of Abraham Lincoln, whom members of the group, like so many of their French compatriots, had idolized.[2] Lincoln was Laboulaye's hero, not only for saving the Union, but for allowing the Frenchman to preserve his attachment to the United States and its institutions. As a principled liberal, the professor hated slavery and served as the head of France's antislavery society. A great many of his American friends and correspondents—Laboulaye never traveled to North America—had distinguished themselves as abolitionist leaders. And Laboulaye's antislavery views had played a major role in turning him against his own government. Napoleon III sided with the South in the Civil War in the belief that a divided America would be too weak to thwart his imperial designs on Mexico, to which the French emperor sent an invasion army in 1862. With U.S. slavery abolished and the Union restored, Laboulaye could maintain intact his rosy view of the United States.

After dinner, the professor and his guests discussed ways they could show the North's victorious leaders that not everyone in France had joined their government in opposing them. Laboulaye wanted to combine that effort with a gesture designed to highlight the superiority of the American political system over France's authoritarian one. It was risky to criticize the Bonapartist government openly, but opponents could attack it indirectly by extolling the merits of another, better place. We don't know exactly what Laboulaye's liberals decided that evening, since no one said anything about it until twenty years later. Only then, in a short fund-raising pamphlet, did Bartholdi explicitly trace the origin of the Statue of Liberty to the dinner of 1865 chez Laboulaye.[3] Most readers took the sculptor's comments to mean that the professor and his guests had decided at that event to create a statue as a gift from France to an American republic soon to celebrate its hundredth birthday. What Laboulaye actually said, according to Bartholdi, was both more tentative and less unilateral: "If a monument should rise in the United States, as a memorial to their independence, I should think it only natural if it were built by united effort—a common work of both our nations."[4] The monument was not to be a gift from France to the U.S., but a common effort of two peoples equally devoted to liberty; the Frenchman acknowledged ruefully that only America enjoyed this freedom.

The idea of a statue of liberty in connection with Lincoln and the United States had in fact surfaced in France in 1865, but not at Laboulaye's summer home. Shortly after news of the president's assassination reached the other side of the Atlantic, a provincial paper, *Le Phare de la Loire* (the *Loire Lighthouse*) took up a collection for a gold medal dedicated to Mary Todd Lincoln. Bartholdi, along with other prominent French artists and intellectuals, helped publicize the fund-raising campaign, which Napoleon III's government tried unsuccessfully to suppress.[5] Money poured in from around the country, and the finished medallion bore the inscription "Dedicated [to] Lincoln, the honest man, who abolished slavery, restored the union, and saved the Republic *without veiling the statue of liberty.*"[6]

Did Bartholdi amalgamate these different elements—the medallion campaign and the dinner party—perhaps without realizing it, twenty years after the fact? Since no gift emerged from Laboulaye's group, and Bartholdi didn't mention a sculptural project for the United States until 1870, it's likely that the idea took some years to germinate in the artist's mind. The delay can't be attributed to a lack of models. Goddesses of liberty, first represented in ancient Rome, resurfaced in profusion during the French Revolution and paraded throughout France from one end of the nineteenth century to the other.[7]

Perhaps the most famous of these female "liberties" stands at the center of Eugène Delacroix's 1830 painting *Liberty Leading the People to the Barricades.* The canvas refers to France's Revolution of 1830 and portrays an allegorical "liberty," or "Marianne," as she came to be known in France, waving the flag of revolution amid a battle scene that features bourgeois and plebeian men united in the cause of freedom. Leading the charge, Marianne towers over the male fighters, her breasts bared and arm aloft sweeping the light of liberty into a halo that illuminates her entire form. This image became an icon of revolution, a collection of symbols whose Phrygian cap, ardent motion, and partial nudity conveyed a message of radicalism. The Phrygian cap, borrowed from ancient Rome, represented the liberation of the enslaved and oppressed, while motion and nudity stood for the ferocious phases of the French Revolution. After the overthrow and execution of the king in 1792–93, goddesses of liberty came to symbolize the new republic that emerged. But the juxtaposition of

Eugène Delacroix, *Liberty Leading the People*, 1830.

terror and the reaction against it produced two kinds of republicanism, one radical and one moderate. The radical version, which Delacroix placed at the center of his painting, made the goddess of liberty a vehement, headstrong figure bristling with mobile energy, just like revolutionaries on the street. Her breasts spilled out from a loose-fitting garment, signaling a natural, Eden-like freedom not without overtones of Eros. Competing with this radical goddess was her far more moderate cousin, a sedate figure who represented the temperate face of French republicanism. This alternative "liberty" stood or sat in one place with a placid expression on her face and her body fully and chastely clothed.[8]

Bartholdi, like Laboulaye, rejected the radical version of French republicanism; his statue would resemble the staid goddesses of liberty that appeared after the Terror of 1793–94, and especially after the Revolution of 1848. These emblems of moderation were designed to calm political passions and steer the country toward a centrist path. One such image, a painting by Ange-Louis Janet-Lange prominently displayed in an artistic competition of 1848, depicted a fully dressed young woman seated and holding a lit torch above her head. Bartholdi must have been familiar with this painting, because he later adapted its title, *La France éclarant le monde* (*France Illuminating* [or *Enlightening*] *the World*), for his Statue of Liberty, which he originally called "Liberty Enlightening the World." Janet-Lange's canvas anticipates the Statue of Liberty's form, as does another image from 1848, this one by Eugène-Andreé Oudiné, which looks even more like the monument Bartholdi would create.[9]

Even if Laboulaye and Bartholdi didn't discuss at the 1865 dinner a monumental gift to the United States, much less a statue of liberty, the sculptor would have had female images of liberty in his head. Such images, as Bartholdi knew, had been familiar to Laboulaye as well. In a pro-Union polemic of 1862, the scholar urged his readers "to range ourselves round [Lincoln and the North], and to hold aloft with a firm hand that old French banner, on which is inscribed, Liberty."[10] In the early and mid-1860s, with liberty stifled in France and threatened in the United States, Bartholdi likely added the goddess of liberty to his artistic and intellectual repertoire. It was a repertoire shaped not by the elite Ecole des beaux-arts, where most talented young artists wanted to study, but by private tutoring and direct access to the leading sculptural ateliers in France. He was admitted thanks to the wealth and connections his family enjoyed.

The Bartholdis (originally Barthold and later Latinized) came from the German Rhineland, where they stood as pillars of the Lutheran church and prospered in business, commerce, and the pro-

Ange-Louis Janet, called Janet-Lange, *La République*, 1848.
(The Image Works, Inc.)

fessions. The family moved across the Rhine to the province of Alsace not long after the territory had passed from German to French hands. They ultimately settled in Colmar, where the Bartholdi mansion still stands as a private museum dedicated to the sculptor's life and work. Auguste Bartholdi's father, Jean-Charles, was a successful civil servant whose land and real estate holdings made him a wealthy

Eugène-Andreé Oudiné, "Medal of the Republic," 1848.

man. After his early death in 1836 (Auguste was born in 1834), his widow, Charlotte, capably managed the family fortune, earning enough to shield her son from all financial concerns.[11] Auguste could pursue his work without having to seek commissions from either private individuals or the state. But his professional autonomy came at a cost. Throughout his life, he remained financially and emotionally dependent on his strong-willed, domineering mother, to whom he wrote faithfully and frequently until her death in 1891.

These letters tell us much of what we know about the conception and planning of the Statue of Liberty, its various fund-raising campaigns, Bartholdi's friends and relations, and his thoughts about his work.[12] They also reveal how much he depended on his mother's approval and the intensity of his attachment to her. He didn't marry until his early forties, and in his letters home he described his new wife, Emilie Jeanne Baheux, as anything but an object of romantic attention or sexual desire. Jeanne, Auguste wrote, resembled a "cousin," who shows "the challenges of her life and her age." Bartholdi apparently wanted his mother to believe that Jeanne could bear children, presenting her as thirty-six when she was actually forty-seven, but he made it abundantly clear that his wife couldn't possibly outshine or overshadow her. Jeanne "has nothing brilliant about her, and she possesses neither fortune, beauty, musical talent, nor worldly éclat."[13] If this description wasn't enough to reassure his mother, Auguste reported that Jeanne's "only concern is to have your affection."[14]

Bartholdi's well-documented attachment to his mother has led biographers and historians to believe that the sculptor imprinted Charlotte's facial features on the Statue of Liberty, but it's doubtful he did.[15] His letters do not suggest that Charlotte was the model for Liberty, which, had it been true, would have greatly pleased the *grande dame*. Still, there is something of the strong mother in the Statue of Liberty, especially as a highly dependent son might imagine her. She's powerful though unthreatening, asexual but still womanly, at once protective and welcoming. Auguste's friend, the French senator Jules François Bozérian, grasped a fundamental truth in maintaining that the New York monument stood as a "work of filial piety."[16] In any case, the strong mother imagery quickly took hold. Already in 1883, Emma Lazarus's poem, "The New Colossus," later to be indelibly associated with the Statue of Liberty, described the monument as a "mighty woman" and "mother of exiles."

Lazarus's poem made explicit the sculptural lineage to which the

Statue of Liberty belonged: the colossi first erected in ancient Egypt and Rome and revived during the Renaissance, thanks in part to the Medicis' desire to symbolize their wealth and power. In the early nineteenth century, artists turned once again to the colossal in the form of Napoleonic grandeur and outsized icons of a new German nationalism.[17] One of Bartholdi's mentors, Antoine Etex, had sculpted two of the giant bas-reliefs that adorn Napoleon's monumental Arc de Triomphe, which ranked as the world's highest triumphal arch (160 feet) until 1982, when North Korea built a slightly taller one for Kim Il-Sung's seventieth birthday.

It's possible that Bartholdi first associated colossal sculpture with reverence for America while under the tutelage of Etex, who idolized the United States and would have familiarized his pupil with the real and mythical colossi of the ancient and Renaissance worlds. Particularly significant was the legendary Colossus of Rhodes, famously depicted in an engraving of 1725 by Fischer von Erlach. Here, a huge male figure stands astride the entrance to the harbor of Rhodes. He holds a smoking torch aloft and wears a crown of spokes not unlike the Statue of Liberty's diadem. Bartholdi called this ancient figure "the most celebrated colossal statue of antiquity."[18] Beyond this classical image, Bartholdi, like all art students of his age, would have known Michelangelo's huge, if not colossal, *David*, and the French sculptor later photographed G. B. Crespi's *St. Charles Borromeo*, a seventeenth-century statue that took nearly a century to build and that rises seventy-five feet atop a pedestal of another forty feet. Finally, Bartholdi acknowledged the influence of two monuments to German glory and the nineteenth-century project of national unification: Ludwig Schwanthaler's ninety-foot *Bavaria* (1848) and Ernst von Bandel's *Arminius* (1875), a gigantic 172-foot monument commemorating the Barbarian hero who annihilated the advancing Roman army in AD 9 and attempted to unite the main Germanic tribes.

Fischer von Erlach, *Colossus of Rhodes*, 1725.

Discussing the merits of colossal statuary, Bartholdi's friend and collaborator E. Lesbazeilles wrote, "That a statue of great size must offer wider meaning, and partake in character of the ideal, is so well understood by the sculptors of our own day that they have almost always reserved the form either for the portrayal of symbols, or for the depiction of personages who belong as much to legend as to history, and are destined to become symbols themselves."[19] Bartholdi's artistic milieu and historical era had primed him for the creation of such symbols, which helps explain the genesis of the Statue of Liberty and why, for the French sculptor, only a colossus could represent the Franco-American connection he hoped to both deepen and commemorate.

Bartholdi's first professional foray into colossal statuary came in 1855, when he unveiled a huge bronze statue of the Napoleonic general Jean Rapp. The piece stood so high—nearly twenty-five

Ludwig Schwanthaler, *Bavaria*, 1848.

feet—that it couldn't fit inside the exhibition hall. The Salon jury decided to show it outside, making Bartholdi a famous man. The following year he took a long, arduous trip up the Nile, where he marveled over the Colossi of Thebes (Luxor today), the two stone statues of Middle Kingdom pharaohs built more than three thousand years ago. Describing these sixty-foot-tall towers of rock, Bartholdi wrote, "We are filled with profound emotion in the presence

Ernst von Bandel, *Arminius*, 1875.

of these colossal witnesses, centuries old, of a past that to us is almost infinite. . . . These granite beings, in their imperturbable majesty, seem to be still listening to the most remote antiquity. Their kindly and impassible glance seems to ignore the present and to be fixed upon an unlimited future."[20]

Bartholdi wanted to chisel colossi of his own, and, like the great sculptors of ancient times, he chose Egypt as his site. In 1869 Khe-

Colossi of Thebes. (B. Anthony Stewart/National Geographic Stock)

dive Ismail, Egypt's westernizing ruler, agreed to see the French sculptor, who proposed to build a mammoth statue at the southern end of the newly opened Suez Canal, built by another Frenchman, Ferdinand de Lesseps.[21] Bartholdi's monument would embody Egypt's new role as linchpin between East and West. Although Ismail proved noncommittal, Bartholdi produced a series of drawings in which the proposed statue began as a gigantic female *fellah*, or Arab peasant, and gradually evolved into a colossal goddess that resembled the ones he had contemplated in the early and mid-1860s. If the original sketches already recalled his mentor Ary Scheffer's republican goddess of 1848, Bartholdi's final drawing for the khedive bore an uncanny likeness to what we know as the Statue of Liberty. Perched atop a high pedestal, the colossus, draped in loose-

Frédéric Auguste Bartholdi, *Egypt Carrying the Light to Asia*, c. 1869.
(Musée Bartholdi, Colmar)

fitting robes, holds a torch high above its head. As a beacon, it would light the way for oncoming ships, and Bartholdi told the khedive it would symbolize "Progress," or "Egypt carrying the light to Asia."[22]

We don't know whether the khedive ever considered Bartholdi's project seriously, but it's likely that he couldn't afford it. The Egyptian ruler had already overspent himself and his kingdom into a mire of debt; there would be no colossal lighthouse at the tip of the canal. Bartholdi returned to France without a commission and at a professional dead end. He eventually decided to develop a series of patriotic sculptures to commemorate French greatness and the country's historical resistance to invaders. Meanwhile, the election of Ulysses S. Grant as U.S. president in 1868 momentarily cheered Laboulaye and his circle of French liberals, who considered the former Union commander a great abolitionist and potential friend to France. But Grant and a majority of Americans seemed to prefer Germany to the homeland of Lafayette. Since the American revolution, and even before, Germans had migrated in large numbers to the United States, making German the United States' second language and giving German Americans considerable influence in Washington—far more than any spokesmen for France.[23]

This situation increasingly worried Laboulaye, who feared that the United States' pro-German orientation would deter his country, long plagued by a seesaw of revolution and reaction, from emulating the orderly democracy and balanced Constitution he so admired in the United States. He also worried that America's economic dynamism and growing international strength would connect it more to Europe's dominant economic powers, Britain and Germany, than to France. The desire to prevent his country's European rivals from monopolizing economic relations with the U.S. made Laboulaye all the more eager to offer a gesture of French goodwill and friendship toward this awakening power. The professor wanted at once to remind Americans of their debt to France, whose financial and military help contributed to the American revolution's success, and to convince them of the economic and cultural advantages of close relations with his homeland.

Unfortunately for Laboulaye, a great many of his compatriots rejected his views; members of the cultural elite remained unconvinced that the United States represented a model for them. In 1867, two of France's most prominent writers, Jules and Edmond de Goncourt, denounced what they took to be America's worship of science and technology at the expense of art and culture and condemned the United States' growing influence over their country. They criticized the Paris International Exposition (world's fair) of that year as "the final blow in the Americanization of France, industry triumphing over art, the steam engine reigning in place of the painting."[24] French commentators who traveled to the New World during this period leveled equally harsh critiques. Alexandre Zannini found America riddled with racial prejudice, hostile to immigrants, and suffering from sharp social inequalities. Meanwhile, Louis-Laurent Simonin, also unsympathetic to the U.S., encountered little love for France among the Americans he met.[25] Such realities appear to have escaped Bartholdi, who stayed in contact with Laboulaye and remained faithful to his ideals.[26]

Both men maintained faith in the United States until 1870, when the Franco-Prussian War of that year dashed their hopes—at least for a time. That conflict, which the German chancellor Otto von Bismarck wanted and Napoleon III foolishly initiated, resulted in the Prussian occupation of large swaths of France, the encirclement of Paris, and the seizure of France's easternmost provinces, Alsace and Lorraine. With Bartholdi's hometown of Colmar now in German hands, the sculptor felt himself an exile, his family trapped behind enemy lines. Laboulaye and Bartholdi hoped for American help—or at least sympathy—if for no other reason than the American revolution's debt to France. Instead, the U.S. government sided with Prussia, as did American editorialists and ordinary citizens from one end of the country to the other.[27]

Patriot that he was, Bartholdi soldiered on. He fought to defend Colmar, and when that effort failed, he joined a group of international volunteers led by the famous Italian revolutionary Giuseppe Garibaldi, who had come to France to defend liberty from Prussia's militaristic regime.[28] Outgunned and outnumbered, these forces, like the main French army, retreated south and west toward Bordeaux, where France's newly declared, if highly fragile, republic had taken refuge. The young French leader, Leon Gambetta, had escaped a besieged Paris in a hot air balloon. The Prussian siege, which lasted from September 1870 to January 1871, caused enormous hardship in the French capital, whose residents were reduced to eating horses and then dogs, cats, and—it was rumored—even rats. This suffering expressed itself first as a fierce, patriotic anger against the Prussians and then as working-class antagonism against a French government blamed for leaving at Bismarck's mercy those Parisians too impoverished to escape the city. The antagonism sharpened when the government, now ensconced in Versailles, signed a "shameful" peace treaty with the German chancellor in early 1871.

The result was a huge urban insurrection, a civil war pitting Paris against the provinces, urban workers against rural landowners and the comfortable bourgeoisie. This Paris Commune, as rebel leaders called it, appeared to announce the class warfare Karl Marx had advocated since the 1840s, and it terrified property owners, solid citizens, and the bulk of provincial France. After ruling Paris for slightly more than two months, the Commune fell to an invasion launched from Versailles and planned by a broad coalition of monarchists, Bonapartists, and conservative republicans. Laboulaye and Bartholdi belonged to the latter group; for them the Commune marked a return to the French revolutionary violence that made them despair of their country's future and admire America's apparent republican moderation all the more.

Laboulaye was, at least, safely ensconced in his country retreat near Versailles, but Bartholdi almost literally found himself without a home. The Germans made it difficult for French citizens who had left Alsace to return there after the war, and in any case, enemy soldiers were billeted in the sculptor's house. He traveled there briefly in May 1871, but to stay would have meant becoming a citizen of the new German Empire, something he couldn't possibly do. At the same time, Bartholdi wanted no part of the Paris Commune, which made his Left Bank apartment off-limits and perhaps out of reach. As for Versailles, this too seemed alien ground, as it was in the great chateau's legendary Hall of Mirrors that Bismarck had announced the creation of his victorious Second Reich. "At the end of the war," Bartholdi wrote, "I couldn't go to my home province, since the Germans had excluded me, while in Paris, the Commune was in full force and civil war at hand."[29] A political exile in his own country, the sculptor resolved to head for the United States.

Did he plan to emigrate there for good? We know, of course, that in the end he didn't, but he may well have entertained the possibility. He arrived in New York with the inflation-adjusted equivalent of over $40,000 in his pocket—not an insignificant sum.[30] The woman he would marry in 1876, whom he had doubtless met while still in France, traveled to the United States at about the same time as he, although she took up residence in Montreal, not New York. Whatever his long-term thoughts, Bartholdi made it clear in the spring and fall of 1871 that he couldn't remain in France. As he told one friend, "Discouraged by everything and finding my ancestral lands prussified, I resolved to travel to the United States."[31] Before leaving, Bartholdi wrote Laboulaye that he had just reread his works on the United States and that he would "try to glorify the Republic and Liberty over there, while waiting for them to be restored one day in our own country—if ever that can happen."[32]

Once the Paris Commune fell in late May 1871 and the moderate liberal Adolphe Thiers took the political reins in France, the sculptor likely felt a measure of relief over his country's political future. His larger concern at that moment may well have been the fate of his "prussified" Alsace. During a stealthy visit to his mother in Colmar, Bartholdi expressed a bitterly wounded Alsatian patriotism by sketching a sculpture titled *The Curse of Alsace*. The work shows a woman prostrate beside a dying child, a grimace of anger and vengeance on her face. At about this time, Bartholdi conceived a funerary memorial to Alsatian national guardsmen killed defending their province, and in 1872 the mayor of Belfort asked him to create a monument commemorating the city's heroism in fighting off the Prussians. Belfort had distinguished itself as the lone Alsatian town not to fall to enemy troops. The result was the *Lion of Belfort* (1880), Bartholdi's most admired work after the Statue of Liberty. The sculpted lion, which Bartholdi had earlier conceived as the symbol of Napoleon's defense of Paris in 1814, now became the emblem of Alsatian fortitude and hope for the future. Set in a citadel overlooking Belfort, the Lion is wounded but appears to growl with defiant rage. With this Alsatian context in mind, José Marti, the Cuban independence fighter and friend of Bartholdi, later wrote that the sculptor had intended his Statue of Liberty "to demand Alsace back for France rather than to illuminate the freedom of the world."[33]

If Marti's comment exaggerates the role Alsatian patriotism played in the genesis of the Statue of Liberty, it suggests nonetheless that the monument's origins lay in a tangled web of thought and design: moderate liberal ideology and iconography; the example of ancient colossi; French idealization of the United States and the wish to mark the abolitionists' success; the abortive Suez lighthouse project; and Bartholdi's Alsatian pride and self-exile to the United States. The statue's origins were at once very French and highly personal to the sculptor himself. Bartholdi doubtless had little conscious awareness of all these sources, and when he first explained the Statue of Liberty's genesis in the pamphlet of 1885, he overlooked or downplayed several of them. In any case, it is likely that what would become the Statue of Liberty began to take shape in Bartholdi's mind on the eve of the Franco-Prussian War of 1870–71.

After returning from Egypt without a commission in the fall of 1869, Bartholdi apparently decided to transform his Egyptian colossus into a neoclassical Statue of Liberty. Art historians have found a series of sketches and clay models apparently done between the spring of 1870 and the spring of 1871 in which the Egyptian figure gradually became Roman and Greek. Whether Egyptian or neoclassical, all shared an up-stretched arm, usually but not always the right arm, holding a torch. The other arm is down by the waist. In some models, especially the Egyptian ones, the breasts are prominent; in others, they are barely visible. Ultimately, Liberty emerged as far more androgynous than her khedival ancestor. And as she left her Egyptian roots behind, she shed her North African dress for the draped garments of ancient Greece. Although the source of light ultimately shifted from her crown to her torch, sketches from the mid-1870s still show beams of light radiating from Liberty's head. But by mid-1871, the statue's headdress became a diadem with seven ray-like spokes, said to embody the Masonic symbolism of the enlightening sun. The rays projected outward toward the Earth's seven continents. Other newly added symbols included the broken chains of slavery trampled under Liberty's feet and, to emphasize the point, another broken chain in her left hand.

In the final sketches and the statue's definitive model, the chains underfoot shrank to the point of near invisibility, and the one in her left hand gave way—at Laboulaye's behest—to a Ten-Commandments-like tablet of laws bearing the inscription "July 4, 1776." By 1871, emancipation was an accomplished fact and America's Reconstruction regime too immoderate for Laboulaye's taste. The cautious professor disliked the Radical Republicans' use of federal power to deprive former Confederates of citizenship rights while abruptly extending such rights to all adult black men. Under Laboulaye's influence, the Statue of Liberty's early meaning as symbol of abolition surrendered to a new significance as sign of the return to normalcy, to American's republican continuity since 1776, to the restraining authority of its Constitution, and to the majesty of its law.

Bartholdi didn't write about the process of turning the Suez lighthouse into the American colossus of liberty—in fact, he later denied any connection between the two—so it's impossible to know how deliberate the process of transformation was.[34] What is clear is that by the time he boarded ship for the United States on June 10, 1871, the transformation was largely complete. He set out for New York with one, and perhaps two, models of the colossal statue in honor of American liberty he intended to build. In the course of his New World journeys, which lasted almost six months, Bartholdi outlined the great symbolic ambitions he held for his colossus and tried to convince influential Americans to support what must have seemed to them, at least at first, an impossibly grandiose idea. That he ultimately succeeded testifies not only to his brilliant salesmanship, but to the statue's ability—even while still on the drawing board—to become what a wide variety of Americans wanted it to be.

TWO

Paying for It

Those who have told the history of the Statue of Liberty have commonly criticized the United States for failing to see the monument's virtues immediately, for being reluctant to contribute to its expense, and for delaying its construction for a decade. Such criticisms are unfair.[1] With hindsight, we know what an extraordinarily successful piece of public statuary Liberty has been, but none of this was evident in June 1871, when the virtually unknown Auguste Bartholdi arrived in New York. Rather than shake our heads over the imaginative failings of Americans in the Gilded Age, we should marvel at the ability of Bartholdi and his allies to transform, in the space of fifteen years, a small clay model into the world's largest statue and place that statue in one of the most prominent locations in the world. For comparison's sake, it's important to keep in mind that the Washington Monument, designed by an American architect to honor perhaps the most widely admired figure in U.S. history, took thirty-six years (1848–85) to build. The Lincoln Memorial took fifty-five years (1867–1922) from conception to realization, and the Roosevelt Memorial twenty-three (1974–97).

When Bartholdi first set foot on U.S. soil, he spoke almost no

English, knew essentially no one, possessed no knowledge of the United States beyond what he had read in Laboulaye's books, and had no American intermediaries to help with his audacious quest. He did have the money to live and travel comfortably here for many months, and he came armed with letters of introduction from Laboulaye to important people in different walks of life. He thus enjoyed advantages denied to most immigrants in search of fame and fortune. Laboulaye had corresponded with a great many Americans— mainly people who shared his moderate liberal politics and abolitionist convictions. It was an impressive but relatively narrow group.

Before arranging to meet Laboulaye's contacts, Bartholdi scouted New York for a place to anchor the statue he had in mind. He visited Central Park, the Battery at the southern tip of Manhattan, and sailed around New York Harbor. He quickly eliminated the park, which then seemed more a suburban green space than an urban sanctuary, and decided that the Battery's dense backdrop of buildings would not give his statue the prominence he desired. Bartholdi turned to the harbor, whose vitality and activity amazed him. "The first thing that strikes the eye," he wrote his mother, "is the immense steamers called 'ferry boats.' . . . They move this way and that across the bay, full of people and covered with flags, emitting deep-toned blasts from their whistles. [The waters] are covered with shipping as far as the eye can reach."[2] If he were to place his statue in the harbor, this limitless flotilla would circle it every day. Even better would be to build it just inside the bay from the narrows, the thin channel through which all ocean vessels coming into New York must pass. On his second day in the city Bartholdi found his spot: Bedloe's Island, a tiny dot of land occupied only by a little-used military fort. From this perfectly situated island, Bartholdi's colossus would be visible from the city, from the harbor, and, perhaps most important, from every ship sailing from the Old World to the New.

The Frenchman's next task was to organize American support. He was aware of the magnitude of his undertaking and told his mother not to mention his project to anyone for fear he "would appear eccentric, even a little crazy."[3] Understandably, he began with American Francophiles likely to be interested in strengthening Franco-American ties. On his third day in New York he met Mary Louise Booth, whose grandfather was French and who spoke the language perfectly. She had translated one of Laboulaye's books and, most important, edited the magazine *Harper's Bazaar.* He then saw several sculptors familiar with his work, the French consul general, and the editor of New York's French-language newspaper, *Le Courrier des Etats-Unis.* All of these people greeted Bartholdi warmly, but none showed interest in his project. He quickly realized that he lacked a clear rationale for building such a statue and thus couldn't explain why Americans might want it and contribute to its costs. It was at this point that he decided to "speak of his project from a new point of view," and began to assert that his colossus would represent "French society's" gift of a "commemorative monument in 1876."[4] Only after arriving in New York—not at the famous 1865 dinner chez Laboulaye—did Bartholdi conceive of the statue as a gift from the French people commemorating the centennial of the American revolution.

This idea evoked a measure of interest. It was less abstract than a statue honoring "liberty," which could mean almost anything, perhaps even the dangerous "license" associated with anarchism and the bloody Paris Commune. Also, a French gift might help diffuse tense Franco-American relations dating back to 1848. The French revolution of that year had abolished slavery in French colonies, a move that horrified American slaveholders, who feared the French emancipation might be contagious.[5] Once the Civil War broke out, it was Northerners' turn to dislike the French, whose government supported the Confederacy. And partly in retaliation, these same

Northerners sided with the Prussians against the French in 1870. Almost no American, it seemed, remembered Lafayette and France's contribution to U.S. independence. To remedy this situation, Bartholdi began to see his statue as a kind of peace offering, as the centerpiece of an effort to restore Franco-American ties. The monument would celebrate not just the American revolution, but also France's contribution to it. The sculptor hoped that Americans would look at his Statue of Liberty and understand their essential, existential ties to his country.

But optimist that he was, even Bartholdi couldn't sustain those hopes. His initial meetings convinced him that gratitude eluded most Americans; they were too focused on "business" (*les affaires*) and the "God Dollar." The American character, he added, "is largely closed to the realm of imagination."[6] And having been schooled on Laboulaye's idealized version of the United States, the sculptor found himself disappointed with the realities he observed. "American life," he wrote his mentor, "seems to allow little time to live—their customs, their regimes are not my ideal. . . . Everything is practical, but in a collective manner. The society marches like rail cars on tracks, but the isolated vehicle is obliged to stay on the rails if it is to move smoothly. The isolated individual cannot emerge; he is obliged to live in this collective society."[7]

A great many Americans, then as now, would have been surprised by this assessment. But Bartholdi's view of the United States as excessively practical, as governed by a railroad-like regimentation, allowed him to understand the Americans' disinterest in his utterly impractical "dream" of erecting a great statue in New York Harbor. Still, he marveled over America's technical advancement and industrial prowess, and once he began to explain his project as a great modernist technical achievement, he would see more success. Until he did so, all he had to show was a small model of a neoclassical woman, which didn't evoke any distinct American traditions, memories, or emotions. Bartholdi's statue left most Americans cold, which, logically enough, is the way he came to see them. (Later, after meeting with President Grant, the Frenchman described him as "a cold man, like most Americans.")[8]

Undaunted, Bartholdi decided to try his luck in Washington, D.C., where a letter of introduction from Laboulaye earned him an audience with Charles Sumner, the influential Republican senator and former abolitionist stalwart. This meeting went much better than those he'd had in New York. Bartholdi found the senator "a cultivated, intelligent man, who likes France."[9] Most important, "He seems sympathetic to my project." But most others in Washington didn't share Sumner's sentiments. Besides Sumner, the lone bright spot there proved to be a Philadelphian, Colonel John W. Forney, publisher of the *Philadelphia Press*. A committed abolitionist like Sumner, Forney understood Bartholdi's monument to liberty as a symbol of emancipation and promised to help the Frenchman advance his project.

In Forney, Bartholdi had found the American advocate he needed, an influential journalist who could to explain to his compatriots why the sculptor's project was meaningful and important. Taking Bartholdi to Philadelphia, a city the Frenchman found "dirty," Forney introduced him to the Union League Club, a network of wealthy liberal men with members in all the major East Coast cities. The club had formed early in the Civil War to support the Union, advocate emancipation, and achieve political reform through education and appreciation of the arts. Members of the Union Club shared many of Laboulaye's views and held the French professor in high esteem. They gave him an honorary membership in 1863 and praised him for advocating abolition, the Union, and the idea—hardly evident in the turbulent, war-torn 1860s—that the United States provided a model for orderly, law-abiding republicanism. The Union League's belief that the arts could—and should—enlighten a backward citizenry drew them to Bartholdi's patriotic work and to his project for a goddess of liberty. Club members in Philadelphia, and especially New York, would form the nucleus of Bartholdi's U.S. backing and play a major role in the 1880s in making the Statue of Liberty a reality. Their elite status and influential connections helped Bartholdi enormously but hurt him as well. For too long, this relatively small group of wealthy, cultivated, Europhilic liberals narrowed the statue's meaning and kept potential supporters at arm's length. Conservative Americans found the Union League's connections to French republicanism suspicious, even dangerous, while left-wing Americans, who advocated women's rights and the advancement of African Americans, took issue with the orderly and restrained vision of liberty in which most club members believed.

In Philadelphia, the Union League overlapped with the Fairmount Park Commission, which ultimately succeeded in preserving about six thousand acres of open space for those who wanted to "escape from the din of crowded city streets."[10] The commission wanted to dot the park with sculpture and other works of art, and its leaders offered Bartholdi a position as director of Philadelphia's sculptural programs. He declined but agreed to contribute a monument for the 1876 centennial celebration of American independence to be held in Fairmount Park. Bartholdi's contribution was destined to play a major role in the development of the Statue of Liberty and its acceptance by the American public.

But for the time being, Bartholdi received precious little encouragement. In many ways, Forney alone seemed to understand his vision. Frederic Law Olmsted, the co-architect of New York's Central Park, dismissed the idea, as did most other artists, businessmen, and politicians the French sculptor met. Part of the problem was that residents of Philadelphia, Washington, and Boston didn't see what was in it for them. How would they and their cities benefit from a monument erected in New York? Not until the twentieth century would the Statue of Liberty come to represent the United States as a whole.

After six weeks of mostly unsuccessful meetings up and down the eastern seaboard, Bartholdi decided on a strategic retreat. He believed he had planted the seed of the Liberty idea, and though it failed to germinate immediately, it might take root in the months and years to come. President Grant, though noncommittal about the project, suggested that the federal government might be willing to give up Bedloe's Island as a military installation, and in Boston, America's most famous poet, Henry Wadsworth Longfellow, expressed a general enthusiasm for Bartholdi's work, if not necessarily for the goddess of liberty. While his project awaited better times, Bartholdi resolved to travel from one end of the United States to the other, learning firsthand about a country, he now realized, that he knew and understood hardly at all.

His first stop was Niagara Falls, where he seemed as interested in John A. Roebling's 822-foot, double-decked suspension bridge as in the waterfall itself.[11] He proceeded on to Detroit and Chicago, where he marveled over the rapidity with which Americans transformed small villages into large, bustling cities. Boarding trains that now spanned the entire continent, he chugged through the endless Midwestern plains and over the Rocky Mountains, which he found "diabolical." They resembled the eerie peaks of mountains "encountered in fairy tales." In Salt Lake City he met with Brigham Young and expressed astonishment that Mormons apparently treated women well while practicing polygamy.[12] When Bartholdi finally reached San Francisco, he found people there even less interested in his liberty goddess than East Coasters had been. He attributed the Californians' indifference not to the vast continental expanse separating them from New York, but to the lingering effects of a gold rush now more than two decades in the past. The sculptor termed

San Francisco a "Babel" of materialism and greed, a place so devoid of moral education as to preclude any appreciation of art.

In an effort to see as much of the U.S. as possible, he traveled back east along a path different from his earlier westerly one, so that he could visit Cheyenne, Denver, Kansas, Saint Louis, Cincinnati, and Pittsburgh. His five-month-long foray through the United States made him one of the best-traveled Frenchmen in America and acquainted him with a relatively broad cross section of the country and its people. By comparison, Tocqueville's infinitely more famous trip of 1831 seems superficial. Bartholdi returned to France at the end of 1871 with a far better understanding of the U.S. than Laboulaye possessed. The sculptor had made himself known in the New World, even if his liberty project had failed to take hold.

If Americans had shown indifference to Bartholdi's republican goddess, his own compatriots seemed even less keen. The Paris Commune had left a bitter aftertaste for almost everyone and deprived moderate, Laboulaye-style liberty of what little support it had once enjoyed. The massacre of the Commune's supporters (and innocent bystanders) during the "bloody week" of late May 1871 angered and alienated the French left, wedding it all the more to its insurrectionary traditions. For conservatives, the Commune provided yet more evidence that France's republics inevitably led to violence, the destruction of property, and the effort to overturn the social order itself. Their solution was the restoration of monarchy, which might have occurred in the early 1870s had there not been three competing pretenders to the throne—Bourbon (Count of Chambord), Orleanist (Count of Paris), and Bonapartist (Napoleon III's son, Eugène Louis). As for moderate republicans, they were committed to creating a stable republic not through violence, as in the past, but through an orderly constitutional process led by a stable middle class and grounded in the people's consent. In the early 1870s these moderates, whose most cautious members included Laboulaye, enjoyed neither the political strength nor the coherent political philosophy necessary to achieve their aims.

In January 1871, French voters elected a largely monarchist parliament. Two years later a monarchist general, Patrice de Mac-Mahon, who had led the suppression of the Commune, became president of a regime that was republican in name only. Under these circumstances, Bartholdi found precious little interest in a monument to republican liberty, however moderate its iconographic roots. During this period he focused on the kinds of patriotic projects on which republicans and monarchists could agree: the *Lion of Belfort*, *Vercingétorix*, and other commemorations of Alsatian heroism and the sacrifices of the Franco-Prussian War.

Meanwhile, in the United States the press's detailed—though often inaccurate—coverage of the Paris Commune had soured American conservatives and a fair number of liberals on the very idea of French liberty and republicanism, which people on this side of the Atlantic now commonly viewed as steeped in violence and blood.[13] For them Bartholdi's sculpture represented not the conservative republic of the post-Reconstruction era, but the radicalism of French Jacobinism and the revolutionary tradition.

As they had done with earlier French revolutions, Americans used the Commune as a means for representing and thinking through their own political and social conflicts. In the aftermath of the Civil War, when former slaves received the right to vote, a great many Americans displaced onto the Commune newfound reservations about democracy and popular government. The Commune was especially useful for certain northern Republicans whose ardor for black suffrage had cooled but who, as former abolitionists, were reluctant to say so directly. As the radical editor of *Leslie's Illustrated Weekly* explained, criticism of the Commune had become "a pretext for persecutions and violent and irresponsible repression of liberal sentiments . . . here in the United States."[14]

Before long, American writers would discover the Commune's "socialistic Democracy" within the borders of their own country. Explaining the unprecedented strike wave of 1877, Congressman James A. Garfield declared: "The red fool-fury of the Seine" has been "transplanted here, taking root in our disasters and drawing its life only from our misfortunes."[15] Once an inspiration for citizens of the United States, French republican culture now took the blame for social conflict in the United States. Those Americans with left-leaning views continued to admire the French republican tradition, but conservatives never regained their earlier enthusiasm for the French Republic. What distanced them from the French Republic also distanced them from their own.

In France, efforts to abolish the republic and re-create a monarchical regime foundered on the three pretenders' competing claims. No single would-be king drew widespread support or competed successfully with leading republican politicians, who attracted a growing number of votes, especially at the local level. Republicans promised social stability, individual liberty, limits on the power of the Catholic Church, and a government staffed not by people with inherited wealth and power, but by individuals of modest background who had worked hard and earned the people's confidence. By 1875 the French parliament leaned republican, and by 1877 Mac-Mahon had no choice but to invite genuine republicans to join the cabinet. The marshal finally resigned in January 1879.

Now, in the second half of the 1870s, to Laboulaye and Bartholdi France seemed ready for their monument to liberty, which the professor had baptized "Liberty Enlightening the World." In 1875, with Mac-Mahon still in office, there was no chance of receiving any government money for the project, so Laboulaye decided to raise the needed funds through private donations. The task would not be easy, as Bartholdi had developed truly colossal plans: his statue would be the largest in the world, a work of engineering as much as a work of art. It would be expensive—initial estimates valued its cost at more than 400,000 French francs (more than $2 million today), not including the pedestal, for which the Americans would be asked to pay. (The ultimate cost was more than double the original estimate.)

The first step in the fund-raising process was to form a committee, dubbed the Franco-American Union, to direct the effort.[16] Its members embodied the moderate republicanism of the new French regime and included descendants of Frenchmen famous for their ties to the United States: Oscar de Lafayette, Hippolyte de Tocqueville, Paul de Remusat, and Jules de Lasteyrie (the latter two related to Lafayette). Laboulaye presided over the group, and the Philadelphian John Forney was an honorary member. These men, and especially the lesser-known names on the committee, resembled adherents of the American Union League Club as much as people from two different countries possibly could. The Frenchmen and Americans alike all were wealthy, moderately liberal, cultivated, and emotionally and intellectually attached to the country on the opposite side of the Atlantic.

Laboulaye and Bartholdi thought it would take a year to raise the money, and, starting as they did in 1875, the two men hoped to have a statue ready in time to celebrate the centennial of American independence. Their timetable proved wildly optimistic; it took five long years to amass the money they needed. At first glance, the slow progress seems unsurprising. After all, the French people were being asked to donate money for a gigantic, expensive statue to be given to a foreign country whose leaders and opinion makers had mostly favored France's enemy in the recent Franco-Prussian War. Worse, the campaign began just as the country fell into a long economic depression and found itself eclipsed in world markets by Britain, Germany, and the United States. Still, for a country as large as France, 400,000 francs represented a relatively small sum. If every family gave the equivalent of a dime, the Franco-American Union would have collected more than enough money. And thanks to a large, powerful, and expanding French press, the Union enjoyed extraordinary visibility. Laboulaye and Bartholdi had shrewdly thought to enlist the country's newspapers, writing personal letters asking for their cooperation. Most editors seemed happy to advertise the fund-raising effort and follow its progress. Ironically, it may be because the Union appeared to enjoy so much support and could boast the endorsement of Lafayettes and Tocquevilles and other members of the French elite that ordinary people, even relatively prosperous ones, felt they didn't need to contribute.

The Union's announcement of its fund-raising drive took the form of an elegantly printed two-page circular, with a triptych of images at the top: a drawing of the statue on Bedloe's Island flanked by portraits of Washington and Lafayette. The statue had seven rays of light glowing outward from its crown. The appeal itself began by proclaiming, "[American] independence . . . marked a turning point in the history of humanity." For the New World, it represented "the founding of a great republic." For France, it embodied one of the "most honorable moments in our history." The circular claimed, against all evidence, "the United States likes to remember its ancient fraternity of arms, and people there honor the name of France. The great event that they will commemorate on July 4, 1876, will allow us to join with our brothers in America in celebrating the old and great friendship that has long united these two peoples."[17] To this wishful thinking Laboulaye, who wrote the text, added that "a French artist had captured the ideas of 1776" so perfectly that everyone in the United States has endorsed his project and "prepared all the means necessary to execute it."

Nothing could be further from the truth, as Laboulaye well knew. Nor was it true, as the circular claimed, that although the French were taking the initiative, "it will be widely reciprocated on the other side of the ocean," or that "the monument will be executed in common by the two peoples." In 1875, this text represented Laboulaye and Bartholdi's hopes and dreams rather any concrete commitments or prospects, and it revealed the fears underlying their project: that the United States would continue to distance itself from France. A central purpose of the Liberty endeavor was to enable France to "occupy the first place in the memories and affections of the United States."

One of the first French newspapers to publicize Laboulaye's appeal was *Le Petit Journal*, the country's best-selling daily and perhaps the most successful paper in the world, with a circulation of 350,000 in 1875.[18] Its political orientation was moderately republican, but *Le Petit Journal*, Europe's first penny paper, was more a commercial than a political venture. Its editors wanted to sell as many copies as possible, and that meant avoiding political controversy and focusing on issues and events likely to enjoy, or evoke, a broad consensus. Bartholdi's Liberty seemed one of those issues, which is why the paper's editorial nom de plume, Thomas Grimm, not only published the Franco-American Union's fund-raising announcement, but framed it with a front-page opinion piece strongly endorsing the venture. "The marquis de Rochambeau and the marquis de Lafayette were the generals who led the glorious phalanges of French fighters who crossed the sea in quest of liberty. . . . Today the grandsons of these illustrious men want to demonstrate to the United States the enduring friendship of France." They did so by "offering America what the French genius can always provide: a work of art." The project's political significance for France was clear. Napoleon III's empire, Grimm wrote, "had cooled relations with the United States by showing a barely disguised sympathy for the secessionist states of the South. Today we have a perfect occasion to make the Americans forget this dynastic intervention; we must not squander this opportunity." The editorial described the statue as if it already existed and concluded, "All French people, regardless of political affiliation, will support this international work."[19]

There were commercial and diplomatic reasons for good relations with the U.S., but even more important, wrote the editors of another moderately republican paper, *Le Bien Public*, was to turn France away from its destructive fixation on Germany and toward peaceful cooperation with America. France had built so many memorials commemorating the Franco-Prussian War that the French public and politicians had become too intent on exacting revenge against Germany. Wouldn't it be better, *Le Bien Public* asked, to take a different kind of revenge, a pacific revenge that would rehabilitate France not by nourishing old hatreds, but by "uniting more closely with our natural allies, both old and new." The U.S. is foremost among these "natural allies," thanks to "France's cooperation in the liberation of America—one of the greatest feats in our nation's history." Many Americans have forgotten this past, the editors said, and the great accomplishment of the Franco-American Union is to have "taken the initiative in building a monument that will perpetuate the memory" of France's role in founding the United States. The Statue of Liberty would be what the contemporary French historian Pierre Nora called a *lieu de mémoire*, a place of memory where Americans would recall what France had done for them and be moved to reciprocate by forging close bonds between the two states.

These and many other French newspapers faithfully covered the subscription campaign, giving Laboulaye's committee a huge amount of free publicity. But the most pivotal coverage may have come from France's growing number of illustrated magazines— many highly popular and increasingly within the financial reach of those with modest incomes. In early October 1875, *Le Journal*

La Statue de la Liberté

QUI DOIT ÊTRE OFFERTE À L'AMÉRIQUE PAR LA FRANCE ET ÉLEVÉE DEVANT NEW-YORK

Dessin de HENRI MEYER d'après les photographies de PIERRE PETIT — Voir les détails, page 323

Engraving depicting how the Statue of Liberty would appear once installed on Bedloe's Island (*Le Journal Illustré*, October 10, 1875).

Illustré published an engraving of the Statue of Liberty, representing how it might look once built on Bedloe's Island.[20] The widely read pictorial weekly *L'Illustration* published the same image, as did *Harper's Weekly* in the United States about six weeks later (November 27). The actual monument would, of course, be quite different in its details—the seven rays of light eventually gave way to a diadem with seven spokes; the torch became much more elaborate; Liberty's left hand took hold of tablet of laws; the pedestal changed dramatically. But this drawing and others like it appeared in French and American illustrated journals so often that the statue's construction seemed to many a fait accompli long before the Franco-American Union actually raised the funds required to build it. One additional reason fund-raising proved so difficult might have turned on the existence of all these drawings. They lent the statue such an aura of reality and inevitability that a great many ordinary people may not have understood why anyone needed their contributions. In fact, most of the money ultimately came from a tiny elite of the French public: leading politicians, bankers, businessmen, and municipal governments. But what they contributed wasn't nearly enough, even when one benefactor, Pierre-Eugène Secrétan, donated much of the copper—64,000 francs worth—needed for the statue. The rest, as we'll see, had to come from the sale of trinkets and souvenirs and a variety of other gimmicks.

If most republican papers supported the statue, conservative periodicals proved more skeptical. *Le Figaro*, a witty, stylish paper that attracted artful writers and reported on high society, doubted that Bartholdi's project would make Americans friendlier to France. "Had the initiators of this impressive project," the editor declared, "taken the trouble to scan the American newspapers . . . they would have perceived the true sentiments of the Americans vis-à-vis the French people, especially since [the recent war]." France's would-be friends in the New World, *Le Figaro* added, "very generally favor Germany" over us.[21] Despite such pessimism, *Le Figaro* was hostile in principle not to the Statue of Liberty, but just to its utility in improving Franco-American relations. That a monarchist paper expressed such a benign attitude doubtless had to do with the way Laboulaye now presented the monument—not as a republican gesture, but as a national one, as an act not of republican solidarity with the United States but of a French patriotism designed to bring

French citizens together. In portraying the statue this way, Laboulaye hoped his compatriots would proudly unite over their country's contributions to world history and advancement of the arts. The Statue of Liberty would be a sign of French greatness and not a symbol of liberation, or republicanism, or anything that liberals and leftists alone could accept.

The relative lack of controversy surrounding the statue, combined with its extensive journalistic support, made members of the Franco-American Union confident—too confident—that contributions would come pouring in. To add yet more visibility to the effort, Laboulaye and his collaborators staged a series of gala events. The first took place in early November 1875 in a main gallery of the Louvre. Its all-establishment and all-male guests (per custom, wives were not invited) dined in the company of Liberty's luminous image ingeniously projected onto one of the great room's distant walls. As the statue shimmered above them, guests made toasts and heard speeches dedicated to Franco-American friendship, but with French national unity in mind. After the vicious, traumatic Paris Commune and the disastrous Franco-Prussian War, it seemed crucial to moderates like Laboulaye to overcome France's divisions of class, status, politics, and religion. In "Liberty Enlightening the World," the professor declared, "the old France no less than the new can find fulfillment, whether your dreams be of Louis XVI or of the Republic."[22] The only people excluded were the radical leftists who supported the Commune.

As always, Laboulaye and Bartholdi paid considerable attention to the press—including the Anglophone press—whose writers and editors attended the banquet in large numbers. Guests sent a collective telegram to President Grant, and Colonel Forney offered an after-dinner speech during which he advertised the centennial exhibition to be held in Philadelphia the following year. The Statue of Liberty, or at least one part of it, would make its first American appearance there. The Louvre event brought in 40,000 francs, about a tenth of Liberty's estimated cost, and its apparent success earned the support of Elihu Washburne, the American ambassador to France who up to now had been skeptical of the project. He urged the U.S. Secretary of State to have Congress designate Bedloe's Island as the monument's site.

The next great fund-raising event took place in Paris's brand-new opera house, the largest, if somewhat kitschy, theater in the world. This *soirée musicale*, the organizers hoped, would secure the needed sum. The well-known composer Charles Gounod had written a cantata, "La Liberté éclairant le monde," to be sung by an all-male amateur chorus more than six hundred strong and drawn from all walks of life. The idea was to associate the Statue of Liberty with the people at large. Such populist extravaganzas had attracted attention in the past, but by 1875 they were out of fashion. Journalists roundly condemned the performance, finding it undignified and excruciatingly off-key. They were irritated enough by it to ungenerously point to the large number of unsold seats in the vast opera house and mock the stale speeches and the poor musical choices. The musical evening was a flop. Not only had the criticism been unkind, but the fund-raiser netted only 8,000 francs, a mere fifth of what the Louvre banquet had brought in.

Meanwhile, Bartholdi had begun work on Liberty's hand and torch, which he intended to display at the Philadelphia centennial. These first efforts made him realize that he had radically underestimated Liberty's overall costs, which he now believed amounted to nearly a million francs. The new estimate was doubly troubling, because by mid-1876 the Union's money had essentially run out. Bartholdi made plans for the liquidation of the project, agreeing to pay any deficits from his personal estate. When he left France in May to attend the Philadelphia event, even the torch was behind schedule, though Bartholdi hastened to finish it before the celebration's end.

But it was possible, even likely, that the torch would be the only part of the statue ever built. In an editorial laced with irony, the *New York Times* emphasized this point: "Although the arrival of the arm seemed to be a satisfactory pledge that the rest of the Statue would soon follow it, there were a few profound thinkers who held an opposite theory. . . . Had the French sculptor honestly intended to complete the Statue of 'Liberty' he would have begun at its foundation, modeling first the boot, then the stocking, then the full leg in the stocking."[23] In 1876, amid the centennial celebration for which Bartholdi had intended his commemorative monument, the entire project threatened to collapse.

What saved it—at least for the time being—was another of Bartholdi's works, a statue of Lafayette sculpted for the city of New York. This highly traditional piece portrayed the "Hero of Two Worlds" standing in a static, unheroic pose. It didn't represent Bartholdi's most distinguished work. Officials had meant to bury the sculpture in an obscure corner of Central Park, but the Frenchman insisted on mounting it prominently in the vastly smaller and more centrally located Union Square. When unveiled on Lafayette's birthday in early September, the memorial evoked a hearty public response. Several thousand people watched as French and American troops marched down Fifth Avenue toward the Square, where the bronze Lafayette received a twenty-one-gun salute. Ships in the harbor answered with salutes of their own, and suddenly Bartholdi found himself a great American celebrity. Journalists extolled his artistic prowess and associated him with Lafayette, whom they now remembered as an honorary Founding Father. As it turned out, an ordinary statue of a pedestrian Lafayette earned Bartholdi the artistic legitimacy from New Yorkers he had lacked until then. He could now proceed with his extraordinary colossus in the harbor.

This turn in the Frenchman's fortunes coincided with an enthusiastic popular response to the Statue of Liberty's hand and torch

Liberty's arm and torch on exhibit at Philadelphia's centennial celebration, 1876. This photograph was the event's most popular memento.

when it finally went up in the waning weeks of the Philadelphia centennial. Visitors flocked to see it, and they were avid to climb to the top, where they would stand on the platform surrounding the torch and look out over Fairmount Park. Bartholdi didn't hesitate to exploit the exhibit commercially, establishing a souvenir stand where Liberty's elbow would have been. He sold everything from photographs and lithographs to pieces of scrap metal from the torch. A picture of the torch proved to be the centennial's most popular memento, and it earned Bartholdi and his statue a huge amount of attention in the Philadelphia press.[24]

The money raised in Philadelphia enabled Bartholdi to replenish the Statue of Liberty's exhausted building fund and thus to open a new chapter in the fund-raising process. After dismantling the arm and torch in Philadelphia, Bartholdi had it moved to New York's Madison Square, where it generated additional revenue from souvenirs, photos, and fees for climbing to the top. Sending the torch to New York allowed Bartholdi to profit from the long-standing rivalry between the two East Coast cities. Whenever the New York fund-raising effort flagged, as happened regularly in the decade from 1876 to 1886, Bartholdi and his Philly friends would threaten to erect the statue in the city of brotherly love.

When Bartholdi returned to France in early 1877, fresh from his successes in New York and Philadelphia, he resolved to rely less on traditional fund-raising and more on the public's interest in buying souvenirs of the monument and desire to see parts—or facsimiles—of it up close. Although the sculptor didn't begin to build the statue in Paris until the early 1880s, by 1877 it was already extraordinarily well known. Magazines on both sides of the Atlantic had published so many drawings of it, and its arm and torch had been photographed so extensively, that it became a familiar part of the Paris and New York landscape (or seascape). If ordinary people didn't want to donate money to building a monument that for them already seemed to exist, a great many eagerly invested francs and dollars in its manufactured artifacts and in visits to the torch and, later, the head.

Extremely popular as well was an elaborate diorama that gave the illusion of viewing the statue as if from the deck of an approaching ship. Erected inside the Palais de l'Industrie in the summer of 1877, the diorama proved wildly successful. As a journalist explained, "By some incredible feat of *trompe-l'oeil,*" those who enter the diorama "are all of a sudden looking out over the stern of an American steamboat on her way out of New York harbor. Very near you, on the bridge, are life-sized people, dressed Yankee-fashion, smoking and talking. . . . All around us, on the choppy waters . . . the traffic is unbelievable . . . and now, from her island, rises the gigantic Statue of Liberty, illuminating the world with the rays of her electric beacon. . . . All around is the beautiful harbor; beyond it, the huge city."[25]

Dioramas and panoramas were not new to the last decades of the nineteenth century, but they traditionally had catered to a relatively elite clientele. By the 1870s they had become part of a huge new mass culture of spectacle made possible by the Paris redevelopment of that time. In the early 1850s, Napoleon III and his prefect of the Seine, Georges-Eugène Haussmann, resolved to transform the French capital from a medieval casbah of narrow, constricted streets to a modern metropolis of broad boulevards, monumental buildings, and tree-lined parks. The boulevards fostered movement and circulation, while the broad sidewalks that flanked them encouraged *flânerie*—seeing and being seen. Walking about the city, the flaneur observed the spectacle of urban life, with its café tables, sidewalk performers, barking newsboys, colorful newspaper kiosks, and endless passersby. The new penny papers reported on this spectacle, amplifying it in the process and narrating the crime it partly fostered, as if crime, too, were a spectacle to watch. After reading about murders in the papers, Parisians flocked to see the victims in the city morgue, which became a top tourist attraction at the fin de siècle. If crime could attract tourists, so could celebrities and battle scenes and the exploits of colonial heroes like Pierre Savorgnan de Brazza —hence the popularity of the wax museum and the late-century "O-rama Craze."[26] People couldn't get enough of these visual illusions at a time when life had become cinematic but the cinema did not yet exist. The O-ramas created the impression of seeing first-hand individuals and phenomena that existed in the past, or in some distant place, or, in the Statue of Liberty's case, in a future that visitors could magically glimpse in the here and now.

Bartholdi invested heavily in creating an especially compelling diorama of the Statue of Liberty, and his investment paid handsome dividends. At 1.5 francs during the week and half a franc on Sundays, almost everyone could afford to go. The Liberty diorama proved a huge fund-raising success and provided journalists with yet another occasion to advertise Bartholdi's American gift. Having seen the illusion of the colossus in New York Harbor, tourists were all the more eager to visit Liberty's actual head at the Paris International Exposition of 1878. In advance of the event, newspapers published drawings of seemingly Lilliputian workers crafting the statue's colossal skull. And journalists made a spectacle of its journey from the Monduit workshops, where construction took place, to the Champs de Mars, where the Eiffel Tower would go up a decade hence. "Suddenly, at about eight o'clock in the evening," wrote one commentator, "a colossal head was discerned through the vault of the Arc de Triomphe. . . . It was at once strange and moving to see that, at each turn of the wheels, the head swayed slightly, as though acknowledging the cheers of the inquisitive crowds. . . . In spite of ourselves we tipped our hats to return the courtesy."[27]

As Bartholdi had learned from the torch's display in Philadelphia, the public would want to go inside. For a small fee, he let them climb to the top. One of these tourists was the young Rudyard Kipling, whose *Souvenirs of France* narrated his visits to Liberty's head. "One ascended by a staircase to the dome of the skull and looked out through vacant eyeballs at a bright colored world beneath. I climbed up there often, and an elderly Frenchman said to me, 'Now you young Englisher, you can say you have looked through the eyes of Liberty Herself.'"[28]

These visits paid off, but the statue's costs continued to mount,

Drawing showing the construction of Liberty's head.

and fund-raising lagged behind; when the 1878 International Exposition ended, the Franco-American Union still lacked the funds to build a body for Liberty's head, arm, and torch. Again, the money problems didn't mean lack of French interest in the statue. A cartoon from the satirical weekly *Le Charivari* depicted a general affection for Bartholdi's creation by showing the colossal head in tears as she's carted out of Paris.[29] *Le Charivari*'s image also revealed the beginning of the statue's personification, the inclination of artists

Climbing inside Liberty's head (*Le Monde Illustré*, September 28, 1878).

and writers to bring the hulking metal sculpture to life. More than most public monuments, Liberty would express human emotions via her face and form, and she would even be made to talk.

Such personalization would endure, as would the commercial usage to which Bartholdi unhesitatingly turned. He raised money not only from souvenir photographs and drawings but from terra-cotta models of the statue itself. While photos sold democratically for between 1 and 5 francs apiece depending on their size, the one-meter-tall models fetched $300 in the U.S. and 1,000 francs in

Liberty crying (*Le Charivari*, November 18, 1878).

France. These expensive terra-cotta reproductions, which closely resembled the definitive model Bartholdi had made in 1875, anticipated the cheap souvenir Statues of Liberty later hawked to tourists in New York. The sculptor also thought to sell businesses the right to use his creation in their logos and advertisements. Although a French champagne maker bought the rights early on, Liberty didn't become a staple of advertising until she finally took her place on Bedloe's Island in 1886.

What enabled Bartholdi finally to reach his financial goal was a huge national lottery, a sweepstakes in which ticket buyers could win several of the sculptor's original sketches, valuable pieces of Japanese art, and paintings by Gustave Doré and Alexandre Cabanel, among six hundred other prizes. After five long years of ceaseless fund-raising involving souvenir selling, tourist fees, banquets, musical evenings, and even a national lottery—officially illegal except for causes representing the "public good"—Bartholdi had finally amassed the nearly one million francs he needed. Construction of the Statue of Liberty could now commence. The colossus would take four years to build.

THREE

Building It

In 1875, after years of tinkering with his Statue of Liberty design, Bartholdi shaped his definitive model. It was made of clay and stood four feet tall. A colossal version of this model would eventually go up in New York Harbor eleven years later. As a work of art, the sculpture was banal. There were statues of liberty galore in nineteenth-century France, and Bartholdi mimicked their neoclassical form. Even his symbolism was standard. Broken chains had long represented freedom from bondage; torches commonly stood for enlightenment, as did rays of light; the tablet evoked the majesty and authority of the law. Bartholdi himself admitted that his statue "wasn't a great work of art."[1] But he knew that its formal artistic originality was beside the point.

Above all, the Statue of Liberty is a masterpiece of engineering and technology. Its Greco-Roman drapery masks what was, for the late nineteenth century, a great technical accomplishment. When we look at the Statue of Liberty, we imagine a huge version of an ordinary statue, a solid stone or iron structure firmly anchored into the hard earth of Bedloe's Island. In fact, the statue is far too large to have been made that way, and even if it could have been, Bartholdi would have been unable to proceed as he did, namely to design and build the monument in a Parisian atelier and then to dismantle it for shipment to New York. So what we see is an optical illusion of sorts. In reality, the visible statue is but a wafer of oxidized copper hammered to a breadth of just 3/32 of an inch—slightly thicker than a penny. It could never stand on its own. Instead, it hangs—all 151 feet of it—on an elegant, invisible skeleton of iron conceived by Gustave Eiffel. In a sense, the Statue of Liberty is a modernist Eiffel Tower sheathed in the respectable garb of classical antiquity. It is analogous to the great nineteenth-century train stations whose core structures were shaped from iron and glass but then discreetly hidden behind conventional facades of stone. Urban planners believed the new stations would be too shocking if they weren't made to blend in. The Eiffel Tower, built for the 1889 International Exposition, explicitly broke with this model by uncloaking the Statue of Liberty's wrought-iron skeleton for all the world to see. Eiffel's modern pyramid would stand as a pure display of engineering genius that served no purpose other than to reveal a new form of art—though even he added some unnecessary architectural adornments.[2] It's worth noting that although Liberty's skeleton is invisible from the outside, visitors can see it when they venture inside. A narrow spiral staircase winds around the skeleton's central pylon all the way to the interior of the head. From that vantage point visitors can look out on the harbor through a windowed dome; en route they can admire the extraordinary metal armature that holds the statue up.[3]

In the 1860s and '70s Eiffel had made himself perhaps the world's greatest builder of railway bridges. Most notable are those that span the Douro River in Oporto, Portugal, and the Truyère in Garabit, France. In both, Eiffel pioneered the use of extraordinarily long iron girders, sweeping arches with no center beams, and flexible joints designed to absorb heat and cold and the shock of moving trains. The sweeping arch allowed Eiffel to anchor his bridges in riverbanks rather than in the water, making them at once easier to build and more stable. To manage the brisk winds howling through a deep river valley, Eiffel substituted spindly trusses for the solid iron beams that bridge builders had traditionally used. Trusses are beams pierced with triangular holes through which the wind can blow—unlike solid beams that meet the wind head on and require complex counterforces to keep them in place. Liberty's skeleton is also made of trussed iron pylons, though here the virtue of the truss-work is its relatively light weight and flexibility rather than openness to wind, which buffets the statue's copper skin and only indirectly the trusses themselves.

To create Liberty's skeleton, Eiffel adapted one of his bridge pylons for use as the statue's central pillar. But since he was building one structure to support another, he had to innovate. Perhaps his biggest challenge was to brace the huge copper form against the high winds that sweep through New York Harbor, and to do so while holding together the hundreds of thin copper plates that form Liberty's skin. That exterior, of course, had to be propped up as well, since it couldn't stand on its own. Eiffel attacked these problems by extending a web of lightweight trussed beams out from the central pillar. Those secondary beams stretched toward the copper skin but didn't touch it directly. To hang the exterior on its skeleton, the engineer used a single bolt to attach flat iron bars to the far end of each beam and then to hundreds of points on a fine lacework of copper itself attached to the skin. Since the thin iron bars were flexible and the single-bolt attachments allowed some give, the bars acted like simple springs. These springs absorbed the statue's movement in the wind, ensuring the stability of the central pylon and the truss-work that branched out from it. This ingenious structural system meant that the copper exterior was not attached directly to the skeleton but rather bobbed around it on a great many rudimentary springs. Although each individual spring was relatively weak, by working in concert the ensemble of springs created a superior kind of strength—tough but elastic, rigid and supple all at once.

What was especially innovative about Eiffel's system was that he didn't need to rest the upper parts of the structure on the lower ones, as in most traditional buildings. Instead, he hung the monument's exterior on a strong but relatively lightweight interior system of support. This approach allowed the statue to rise to considerable height while being sturdy and unthreatened by wind. In conceiving it, Eiffel anticipated the architectural principles later used in the skyscrapers of Chicago and New York. He produced, as Marvin Trachtenberg has noted, one of the first "great curtain wall constructions."[4]

The structure nonetheless had to be anchored on the bottom. This Eiffel achieved by having his skeleton stand on four metal plates, each of which would eventually be rooted deep into a stone pedestal erected on Bedloe's Island. Eiffel's final structural problem involved Liberty's up-stretched arm and torch, an appendage that rises almost forty-one feet above the statue's crown. To build it, the engineer lined the arm and torch with an asymmetrical trussed girder delicately attached to the copper skin. Here, Eiffel employed the lessons learned from his bridges to create an appendage that would remain firmly connected to Liberty's upper body without requiring a bulging undercarriage of support that would have ruined the proportions of the sculpture. But during construction Bartholdi or his workmen changed Eiffel's design and in the process weakened the arm, which may, in any case, have required more support. During the statue's first century, engineers had to reinforce it twice (1932 and 1984) to keep it safe. Still, Eiffel's solution was brilliant for its time and allowed visitors to climb to the torch's viewing platform high above Liberty's head. Those making the ascent could feel the entire arm swaying eerily but harmlessly in the wind.

One last engineering matter involved the strong electrical jolts that can occur when sprays of salt water land in places where iron connects to copper. In effect, the Statue of Liberty has the potential to be a 151-foot-tall battery. To prevent it from generating electric currents, workmen had to slide fabrics covered with red lead or made of asbestos inside the iron/copper joints. (Asbestos was banned from construction only in the late twentieth century.) Marine architects had used the same technique in building ships with huge metal hulls.[5] Had Eiffel's genius found a way to harness the statue's electricity-generating power, the lighting problem that long plagued Lady Liberty might have been solved!

If the support structure required engineering brilliance, constructing the gigantic copper sculpture called for extraordinarily careful calculations, an army of highly skilled craftsmen, and the ability to manage the transformation of a four-foot model into a 151-foot colossus. Bartholdi organized the enlargement in three steps. First he magnified the original model into a plaster statue nine feet tall. Then he enlarged that by a factor of four, producing a new plaster model thirty-six feet high. The final step involved another fourfold enlargement to Liberty's full size. The actual monument was so huge that Bartholdi had to produce this final enlargement by dividing the thirty-six-foot model into dozens of sections and then magnifying each of them one by one. This process required nine thousand painstaking measurements for each section and a battalion of expert craftsmen. Bartholdi's men could work on only a few sections at a time, since their workshop, big as it was, couldn't begin to accommodate the entire jigsaw puzzle that Liberty had become. In theory, each enlargement should have been identical to the original, except of course for the difference in scale. But scale mattered, and the magnifications altered the statue's visual effects. Bartholdi constantly had to make corrections, which meant that he was anything but an absentee architect.

His work was at once intricate and grandiose; it took place at the

Gaget and Gauthier workshops (formerly the Monduit workshops) just outside what until 1860 was the northwestern boundary of Paris. Today, this area is ritzy and upper class, distinguished by the elegant Parc Monceau. In the late nineteenth century, the Gaget and Gauthier workshops stood on a no-man's-land between the city and the suburbs that was home to a chaos of warehouses, factories, and makeshift structures. Both geographically and psychologically, it was a long way from the well-kept neighborhoods of central Paris, where Bartholdi lived. Still, as the Statue of Liberty began to rise above the squat rooftops of the city, it became a major Parisian curiosity, and a great many people came to see it.

Honoré Monduit and his successors Gaget and Gauthier employed more than six hundred highly skilled artisans, who embodied the best traditions of French craftsmanship passed down from the Middle Ages. Before devoting nearly full time to the Statue of Liberty, the Monduit workshops did high-quality decorative work for the restoration of the Sainte-Chapelle and Notre Dame cathedrals. Monduit also helped craft the dome for Charles Garnier's splashy opera house, commissioned by Napoleon III and completed just as the Statue of Liberty had begun to take shape. Before bringing in Eiffel as his main engineer, Bartholdi had worked with Eugène Viollet-le-Duc, himself famous for restoring several of France's most notable castles and cathedrals. Although Viollet-le-Duc didn't see the project through (he died in 1879), he influenced the design and conception of Bartholdi's statue.[6]

Never a modest man, Bartholdi knew that his construction project represented history in the making, and he and the photographer Pierre Petit made an elaborate pictorial record of each stage in the process. These photographs allow us to see exactly how the sculptor and his craftsmen built the Statue of Liberty. In addition, an article in the French engineering magazine *La Génie Civile* (1883), for which Bartholdi likely gave detailed information, explained the technical

Plasterers building Liberty's left hand and tablet. (© Collection Musée des arts et métiers [CNAM], Paris/Fonds Bartholdi)

particulars of the construction process. The first step was to create a wood frame for each section of the statue. Craftsmen then plastered the frames to produce an exact replica of each full-size piece. Petit's photographs show pygmy-like plasterers engulfed in a hand or overwhelmed by the scale of the torch or the head. Once plaster versions of each piece had taken shape, workmen undertook the difficult, intricate task of making wood impressions of them. Plaster had to give way to wood, because plaster couldn't withstand the thousands of hammer blows integral to the process of sculpting thin copper sheets. So, each section began with a wood skeleton around which workmen fashioned a plaster model, whose purpose was to provide the form for shaping the necessary wood molds. The final stage in the process involved placing copper sheets, each three to nine square feet in size, on the wood molds and then using large wooden mallets to make them conform to the mold. On sections of the statue with elaborate curves, the copper sheets had to be heated to give them the flexibility required.

Once the copper sheets had been beaten and fired into shape, workmen carefully extracted them from the molds. The last thing they wanted was to distort the forms they had so painstakingly created. Still, as an added precaution, Bartholdi used the plaster models to shape easily malleable, wafer-thin lead sheets into the form of Liberty's skin. He then had his craftsmen press the molded copper sheets onto the lead ones to smooth out any remaining roughness and ensure that the copper conformed precisely to the plaster molds. Since no copper sheet was wider than about four and a half feet, several had to be joined together to produce the completed copper skin for each section of the statue. To keep track of all the sections, molds, and copper pieces, workmen carefully numbered and catalogued every one of them so that those who ultimately erected the Statue of Liberty would know how each piece of the puzzle fit together. By the end of this process, Gaget and Gauthier had produced three hundred separate pieces of Liberty's copper skin. Together they weighed 88 tons (176,000 pounds), which, with the 132-ton iron skeleton, made for a colossus of 220 tons.

The mammoth task of building the Statue of Liberty stretched over eight years, from 1876 to 1884. The statue's size and scale, plus the unprecedented techniques and craftsmanship involved, had attracted enormous attention in the press, as had the five-year-long fund-raising process. As a result, virtually everyone in France, and especially Parisians, could not help but be familiar with the project—all the more so after Bartholdi prominently displayed its head during the Paris International Exposition of 1878. Parisians would have been hugely disappointed not to see the finished product, and Bar-

Liberty's main pylon and secondary structure. (© Collection Musée des arts et métiers [CNAM], Paris/Fonds Bartholdi)

tholdi had always intended that they would. In the summer of 1882 Gaget and Gauthier began assembling the pieces already completed and undertook the task of putting the entire statue together, as if a gigantic Erector set. Again, a series of startling photographs document the process: first the central pylon, then the secondary parts of the inner structure. Before long, Parisians could glimpse the statue itself taking shape, as workmen began to hang the copper skin on its iron frame.

Liberty going up in Paris. (© Collection Musée des arts et métiers [CNAM], Paris/Fonds Bartholdi)

In Liberty's metal girders, Parisians caught a foretaste of the Eiffel Tower, destined to rise just a half-decade later. But with the tower as yet unbuilt, Bartholdi's statue became the French capital's tallest structure. It drew everyone's attention, and when finished, the scaffolding partly dismantled to reveal the head and torch, Liberty Enlightening the World loomed high over the seven-story buildings of Haussmann's Paris. Although widely disseminated at the time, the photograph showing the Statue of Liberty against a Paris backdrop may seem disorienting today to Americans and others accustomed to the monument as a fixture of New York Harbor.

On February 1, 1884, Bartholdi told Richard Butler, chair of the American branch of the Franco-American Union, the so-called American Committee created to raise funds for the pedestal, that the statue was almost done and that he would let it stand in Paris until at least July 4. On Independence Day, he would officially present the French people's gift to the U.S. ambassador in France. Throughout the spring and fall of that year, many distinguished people from around the country paid the statue a visit. President Jules Grévy gave it his country's official recognition in early March, and a half-year later the legendary eighty-two-year-old Victor Hugo saw Liberty in what proved to be the last outing of his life. Afterward he wrote, "I have been to see Bartholdi's colossal . . . statue for America. . . . It is superb. When I saw the statue I said: 'The sea, that great tempestuous force, bears witness to the union of two great peaceful lands.'" Bartholdi had invited his mother and several of his financial supporters to observe the poet's encounter with Lady Liberty, and the banker Henri Cernuschi commented, "I see two colossuses who take each other in."[7] The sculptor gave Hugo a fragment of the statue as a memento, and he later wrote the American ambassador, "Our illustrious poet had tears in his eyes, as did my mother; in short, everyone was deeply moved."[8]

In part, they were moved by the thought of dismantling the statue and having it sent away. Over the previous year, Parisians had become accustomed to its looming presence and to its patriotic and republican symbolism. Many in France wanted it to stay. As the journalist Claude Julien wrote, "It is not without a profound regret that we will see it go. Our patriotism has dreamed of it elsewhere than on the other side of the ocean. We would have liked to see it on the crest of the Vosges, as a memento and a promise, as a response to the Germania of the Niederwald [the 130-foot-tall sculpture commemorating the new German Empire]. To this monument in-augurated by monarchs, the Statue of Liberty would have stood in reply as symbol of republican France."[9] Julien concluded by asking that Bartholdi build another Statue of Liberty for France, which he would eventually do, though at one-quarter of the original's size. This replica, a gift from the American community in Paris to the French people, now stands on a small island in the Seine.

If Liberty represented French patriotism before it stood for the United States, French writers also understood "Liberty Enlight-ening the World" as an expression of their country's scientific and technical prowess, as symbolizing a resurgent and newly confident people who had overcome the military and political humiliations of 1870–71. Bartholdi had shown, wrote André Michel, that France measured up to the world's other great industrial powers and that the country was capable of a "male and noble talent" in science and engineering. France, he said, should not be defined in terms of the female "seductions" of impressionism, "the pretty approximations, the pleasant negligence" of a form of painting temporarily à la mode. Bartholdi's work, by contrast, exhibited a host of male virtues: it was "frank and decisive," "sincere and precise," "profound and durable." Since the disaster of 1871, a great many French commentators had fretted over their country's apparent loss of virility in relation to the Germans. At the beginning of the century, Napoleon had thrashed both the Prussian and the Austrian armies; sixty-odd years later, the Prussians turned the tables on France. It's ironic that Bartholdi's sign of a renewed French manliness took a neoclassical female form, but, for writers like Michel, what counted was Bartholdi's virile per-sistence against all the odds and the engineering genius that had allowed his statue to take shape.

As Julien and Michel expressed the French attachment to Bar-tholdi's work, others doubted that the Americans would appreciate it. "Our Americans," commented an editorialist for *Le Quotidien*, "are too practical to be enthusiastic, like the French, over seeing the Statue of Liberty. Their god is the dollar."[10] One reason for such French negativity stemmed from the apparent U.S. disinterest in accepting Bartholdi's gift. Such, in any case, was the way numerous French writers interpreted the slow pace of the New York fundraising campaign for Liberty's pedestal. Bartholdi himself expressed disillusionment over what seemed lukewarm U.S. interest in his completed colossus. One reason he kept it standing so long in Paris turned on the lack of money for its pedestal—which the Americans had agreed to finance—in New York.[11] Bartholdi waited until early 1885 to begin dismantling the Statue of Liberty from its Paris perch. His workmen packed it into 212 crates, each so heavy that together they required seventy boxcars and sixteen days for the trip to its Normandy port. From there the steamer *L'Isère* took all the pieces to New York. In its lone contribution to Liberty's cost, the French government paid for shipping it across the Atlantic. Once unloaded on Bedloe's Island, the crated statue sat, unopened, for nearly a year.

In 1877, the U.S. Congress had passed a bill agreeing to locate the Statue of Liberty on Bedloe's Island and to accept responsibility for its pedestal. Congress did not, however, appropriate any funds for this purpose. The statue's American backers had to finance this part of the project; they did so by creating the American Committee of the Franco-American Union, designed as the sister organization of its French counterpart. The American Committee's efforts didn't go very well. But New York group nevertheless organized an architectural competition for the pedestal and awarded the commission to Richard Morris Hunt, the first American of his profession trained in Paris at the Ecole des beaux-arts. Hunt was the best-known contemporary architect in the United States, and Bartholdi had sought him out during his initial U.S. voyage in 1871.[12] As a long-standing member of the Union League Club, Hunt belonged to the liberal,

Europhile establishment that had championed the Liberty project in New York and Philadelphia. He had designed homes and offices for its leaders and, in general, for the East Coast's moneyed elite, including Joseph W. Drexel, the wealthy Wall Street banker who later headed the American Committee.

While Hunt worked on his plans for the pedestal, the project's civil engineer, Charles P. Stone, began excavating the foundation to which the pedestal would be attached. Stone had worked for Khedive Ismail in the late 1860s, exactly when Bartholdi had tried to sell the Egyptian ruler on his lighthouse project for the Suez Canal. On Bedloe's Island, Stone left nothing to chance. He sunk the pedestal's foundation to a depth of thirty feet and situated it in the center of a solid pyramidal fortress that had long dominated the tiny speck of land. At its bottom, the foundation measured ninety-one square feet, tapering to sixty-five at the top, where the pedestal would be attached. Together, the foundation and pedestal would slightly exceed the statue in height—153 feet, compared to almost 152 for Liberty herself. For both the foundation and pedestal, Stone and Hunt used twenty-seven thousand tons of concrete reinforced with steel girders just inside its walls. Connected to those girders were huge pairs of triple steel I-beams, which yoked the foundation, pedestal, and statue so firmly together that the builders claimed the only way to topple the ensemble would be to yank the entire island up from its roots.[13]

For Hunt, the pedestal represented several challenges. It had to be grand and monumental enough to fit with the colossal size and ambition of the statue it was to support. But it could in no way overshadow or diminish Bartholdi's monument. The pedestal thus needed to be a distinctive piece of architecture in its own right, while simultaneously drawing the viewer's eye up and away from itself and toward what sat on its roof. Hunt's initial designs failed to achieve this difficult balance; he had sketched a pedestal that was

Richard Morris Hunt's Liberty pedestal.

too elaborate and grandiose. The problems stemmed from the model he had used: the Pharos (lighthouse) of Alexandria, built on tiny Pharos Island between 280 and 247 BC and long one of the seven wonders of the ancient world.[14] Like Bartholdi, Hunt found himself inspired by ancient Egypt; had the French sculptor built his colossus for the Suez Canal, Hunt's initial designs might have produced an ideal pedestal for it. One key problem, though, was that the

Pharos of Alexandra served not to support another, more important, structure, but rather stood as an architectural wonder in its own right. A small statue of Poseidon did cling to the Pharos's top during the Roman period, but the "pedestal" overwhelmed the statue, which seemed essentially a decorative afterthought to a building designed to light the harbor for incoming ships.

Hunt obviously understood that the Statue of Liberty was to be the most important structure on Bedloe's Island, and when he eventually reduced the pedestal's height and width, its proportions complemented rather than diminished the sculpture on top. Still, by retaining the Pharos-inspired Doric columns, arched opening, protruding disks, and coarse, rustic blocks, Hunt avoided an architectural neutrality unsuited to the project at hand. That neutrality belonged to the straightforward, pyramid-like foundation, which Hunt's pedestal linked to the monument as a whole through an ingenious combination of simplicity and grandeur.

By August of 1884, with the foundation well under way, Hunt's revised design had been approved, the pedestal ready to go up. The Statue of Liberty, as Parisians knew firsthand, was ready as well. But Hunt, accustomed as he was to commissions for Fifth Avenue mansions and elaborate "cottages" in Newport, Rhode Island, faced a novel situation. He had no one to pay his bills.

FOUR

American Reticence?

The celebration of the Statue of Liberty's unveiling on October 28, 1886, proved so festive and joyous, attracting more than a million people into the New York streets, that it was easy to forget the myriad problems associated with the monument's reception in the United States. Americans mostly remembered Liberty as "a gift from France," one that became so familiar a U.S. landmark that there seemed no reason to recall the uncertainty surrounding its construction earlier in the decade. Not until after World War II, when scholars began to study the monument's history, did literature on the subject begin to detail the difficult fund-raising campaign for the pedestal, the skepticism about the statue in certain U.S. quarters, and the French irritation over the "ingratitude" of the Americans.

The best postwar books came from French writers, and they tended to echo, however politely, that irritation.[1] But an important early American work by Hertha Pauli and E. B. Ashton also focused on the apparent U.S. reluctance to pay for its part of the monument.[2] Gradually a consensus developed, at least among scholars, that American opinion in the early 1880s was largely hostile to the statue. The view became so entrenched that the excellent catalogue prepared for the statue's centennial exhibition in 1986 had to acknowledge it—while at the same time denying its veracity: "The modern notion that the statue was maligned in the press is a distortion of the truth. Acrimonious jibes and misunderstandings filled the news, but reactions to the gift of the statue itself were overwhelmingly positive."[3]

While it's true that recent writers have exaggerated the American negativity, the U.S. reception was not quite as favorable as the centennial catalogue suggests. This should not surprise. As we've seen, American authorities and civic groups found it difficult to get monuments built in the nineteenth century, and the early 1880s was a time of economic difficulty, with public and private money relatively scarce. Certain industrialists and bankers had, of course, become extraordinarily rich during this period—the Gilded Age—but the newly wealthy had not yet turned to philanthropy, as Andrew Carnegie would do later on. The "robber barons" tended to display their wealth by building great mansions, even castles, for themselves, rather than by giving money to others or by ostentatiously financing great civic projects.

Beyond these historical matters, psychological complexities involved in gift-giving can make individuals, groups, or countries hesitant to accept them. Marcel Mauss's famous *Essay on the Gift* (1924) suggests that gifts can be troublesome because they require a response from those who receive them. The response in question might be no more than an expression of gratitude. But because in many cultures the act of gift-giving places the recipient in one's debt and puts his honor at risk, it is possible that influential, late nineteenth-century Americans sensed the possibility of peril in this unsolicited French offering.[4] After all, we've seen that the French—or at least those associated with Laboulaye and Bartholdi—did want something in return. They wanted the Americans to remember, with gratitude, the French contribution to the war of independence against the British and, as a result, to prefer France to its European rivals in political and economic relations. Bartholdi also wanted Americans to implicitly acknowledge French superiority in the arts by accepting a huge monument conceived and executed entirely by them—albeit with what they perceived to be American ideals in mind. In a mordant satire of U.S. opponents of the French statue, the *New York Times*, though favorable to the project, acknowledged a certain Bartholdian presumptuousness.

> This effort to compel us to pay out of our own money for the embellishment of our harbor has not yet been condemned by the press with the severity which it deserves. . . . There appears to have been an idea among the Frenchmen that we are a people capable of appreciating a graceful and generous act and of taking pleasure in seeing our harbor embellished. Of course, this idea no longer exists. . . . It is, therefore, better to tell the Frenchmen frankly what we think of their conduct and what we feel that we have a right to expect. If they will put up the statue at their own expense, and pay us, say, $10,000 a year as rent for the site on which they place it, we will probably agree not to break it up and sell it for old bronze.[5]

The *Times* editor who wrote the piece clearly had his tongue in cheek, but he nonetheless conveyed a certain ambivalence toward Bartholdi and his project.

Still, whatever the psychological and emotional complexities, the basic problem came down to money. The American backers of Bartholdi's project had agreed to pay for the pedestal, and they proved unable to raise the sum required: nearly $300,000 (over $7 million today), or double the original estimate. The fund-raising campaign started out well enough in 1877, when the committee attracted sizable contributions from John Jacob Astor and Joseph Drexel ($5,000 each, or about $100,000 today). But Cornelius Vanderbilt gave only

$500 and P. T. Barnum just $250. Wealthy New Yorkers seemed unwilling to reach deep into their pockets. Joseph Pulitzer, the flamboyant newspaper publisher, recognized this reluctance as grist for his populist mill: "We have more than a hundred millionaires in this city," he wrote in 1883, "any one of whom might have drawn a cheque for the whole sum without feeling that he had given away a dollar. Any one of whom would have willingly spent the amount in flunkeyism or ostentation [or on] a foreign ballet dancer or opera singer. . . . But do they care for a Statue of Liberty, which only reminds them of the equality of all citizens of the Republic?"[6]

As we've seen, some conservative Americans may indeed have felt no ardent commitment to equality and republicanism, and they likely enjoyed plenty of company in perceiving the French republic as dangerous. On this score, Bartholdi and Laboulaye tried to be as reassuring as possible. During the centennial of the Declaration of Independence, the professor described the French gift, "Liberty Enlightening the World," as representing "Liberty, yes, but the *American Liberty*. It is not that Liberty who, wearing a red bonnet and carrying a pike, marches over a field of dead bodies."[7] Laboulaye's meaning was crystal clear: Bartholdi's statue symbolized the moderate, orderly liberty that French liberals associated with the American republic and not necessarily with its French counterpart. As the Paris Commune seemed to confirm, the French republic too readily, in Laboulaye's view, resorted to violence and a red radicalism that threatened liberty rather than promoted it.

The prosperous businessmen who championed the Statue of Liberty project in the United States and sought funds for its pedestal doubtless understood the statue's symbolism in ways Laboulaye and Bartholdi intended. But perceptions of Liberty's meaning have been anything but stable, and American commentators quickly unmoored it from the two Frenchmen's intentions. Never did Laboulaye and Bartholdi intend it to symbolize an open U.S. door to immigration, as many Americans would eventually come to see it, nor did the two Frenchmen understand the statue as representing the United States itself. For them, it stood for American *liberty*, a universal ideal that stemmed from the U.S. experience but applied everywhere. The United States didn't—and shouldn't—monopolize the orderly liberty it had invented; for that reason, the Statue of Liberty could not symbolize America alone.

Part of the problem for American fund-raisers was that the Statue of Liberty had no precise meaning. It wasn't a likeness of any particular individual, nor did it commemorate a significant historical event, as monuments often did. Its status as a "hollow icon" made it difficult to sell as something essential to the American landscape. The New York *Herald* endorsed Bartholdi's statue of Lafayette for Union Square but found Liberty too "abstract." Compounding the problem was the latter's proposed location in New York Harbor. Residents of other cities and states failed to see why they should contribute to an "embellishment" seen as benefiting New York alone. One Indianan wrote, "Our people will not understand this [the pedestal] as a national matter [but rather as] a New York Affair." And other writers from beyond the era's *New Yorker* map criticized the fund-raising committee for trying to get "the people of Chicago and Connecticut . . . to pay the expense that those of New York would like to avoid."[8] These critics, and the many others who shared their views, could not have known at that point that Bartholdi's sculpture would ultimately represent the United States as a whole; they therefore refused to help finance the pedestal—unless the statue were relocated close to them.

In fact, other cities made bids for the statue when New Yorkers appeared less than enthusiastic about it. As early as 1876, the *Press* of Philadelphia declared, "If it should happen . . . that the citizens of New York should coldly ignore this splendid memorial of Liberty's Centennial, they may be sure that Philadelphia will eagerly welcome it to her beautiful [Fairmount] Park, and there erect it in all its original grandeur.[9] Eight years later, when it looked like the pedestal might not be funded, the *San Francisco Daily Report* staked a claim of its own. "We can give it a site worthy of the ideal [the Statue of Liberty] symbolizes. The Golden Gate, so majestic from every vantage point, offers a natural and appropriate placement for the statue." The people of San Francisco, the paper declared, "are prepared to build the pedestal, and M. Bartholdi has only to say the word and he will see his statue accepted with enthusiasm."[10] Meanwhile, New York newspapers, whose editors mostly supported the monument, worried, as the *Commercial Advertiser* put it, "that Philadelphia or some other city might eventually secure that statue."[11]

Bartholdi took little comfort in Philadelphia and San Francisco's apparent interest; he wanted his statue to reside on Bedloe's Island and stand at the entrance to America's greatest port. Still, in 1882 he made a show of entertaining a proposal from a group of Boston Brahmins to build the statue there. As discussions proceeded, the *New York Times*, now fully committed to Bartholdi's project, slapped the New Englanders down: "This statue is dear to us, though we have never looked upon it, and no third-rate town is going to step in and take it from us. . . . Let Boston be warned [that] we have more than a million people in this City who are resolved that the great lighthouse statue shall be smashed into minute fragments before it shall be stuck up in Boston Harbor." The *Times* went on to plead for more contributions to the pedestal fund and concluded, "Those of us who have pensively contemplated the titanic fist of this statue during its prolonged exhibition in Madison Square are haunted with a desire to see the completed work."[12]

In late 1882 and early 1883, the American Committee redoubled its efforts but still came up short. French commentators reacted sharply to this latest U.S. failure. Americans were too materialistic, editorialists said, to appreciate Bartholdi's work of art, and, in addition, a heavy German influence in the U.S. had supposedly prejudiced Americans against anything French and encouraged U.S. politicians to pander to "Prussian" views. As one French diplomat concluded, "the gift has gotten in the way."[13]

These French views, while perhaps understandable, missed the mark. Those Americans genuinely opposed to the statue took their stand mostly on religious grounds. Some Protestants denounced it as pagan and idolatrous, and the Catholic theologian John Gilmary Shea wrote that Jesus alone, not some Roman goddess, stands as "the true light that enlighteneth the world." The only freedom worthy of its name, Shea continued, is "the freedom wherewith He hath made us free."[14] These, however, were minority views. If most Americans failed to embrace the French gift, they didn't reject it either. Not unlike their counterparts across the Atlantic, ordinary U.S. citizens believed that the wealthy members of the American Committee should pay for the pedestal, especially since many of the gala events associated with the fund-raising effort appealed to the fashionable elites and members of high society.[15]

When even such exclusive occasions failed to raise the required sum, committee members turned to the same measures that the French fund-raisers had used successfully for the statue itself: benefit concerts, art exhibits, and auctions; sales of souvenir photographs, sheet music, and models of the statue; Bartholdi paraphernalia and mementos, including three thousand signatures sold to autograph collectors. Together, these efforts contributed effectively, if modestly, to the fund-raising campaign. One of the most successful among them was the Art Loan Exhibition, for which noted painters and writers donated a work to be auctioned for the pedestal's benefit. It was for this exhibition, held in late 1883, that Emma Lazarus (1849–1887) contributed the poem "The New Colossus."

Decades later, Lazarus's sonnet became indelibly linked to Bartholdi's sculpture, but in 1883 it contributed little to the pedestal fund-raising effort, which once again had stalled. By the end of 1883, the Statue of Liberty stood fully completed on the northwestern edge of Paris, bursting through its workshop and towering over the city as if transported there from a planet of giant women. The statue appeared to wait uneasily in a neighborhood ill suited to house it, while the Americans scrambled unsuccessfully to give it its footing in New York Harbor.

Desperate now, the American Committee appealed to New York's moneyed elite, asking Samuel J. Tilden (the former presidential candidate), Astor, and Vanderbilt for $10,000 each. All three declined. Members of a larger group found themselves solicited for $5,000 each, and most said no.[16] The extraordinary wealth of the individuals in question made these requests perfectly reasonable in financial terms, but in the 1880s most were still involved in amassing money, not in giving it away. And as practical men, they might not have seen the value of this proffered French gift or of its republican symbolism. Pulitzer, as we've seen, maintained that the New York elite had in fact distanced itself from the republic.

Those few prominent figures who explained their refusal to contribute did so on aesthetic grounds. Hamilton Fish, the former U.S. senator and governor of New York who also served as President Grant's secretary of state, believed the statue "neither an object of Art or of Beauty."[17] Mark Twain took the opposite view. He found the statue too perfect, too "hearty and well-fed." He would have preferred a much more tattered monument, one that was "old, bent, clothed in rags, downcast, shame-faced," so it could represent the "insults and humiliation" the principles of liberty have faced over the past six thousand years. Instead, Bartholdi's monument displayed nothing less than "the insolence of prosperity," the forgetfulness of a people whose wealth and comfort have made them take freedom too much for granted.[18]

Although the *New York Times* published Twain's remarks, its editors supported the statue as Bartholdi had conceived it. They did, however, understand the aesthetic objections to it. "If this project had taken a less questionable and more conventional shape," the editors wrote, "it is not probable that we should have dawdled so much over the provision of a pedestal." New Yorkers, the paper added, would have found an obelisk "safe" and provided the necessary funds to situate it quickly. "There was, however, a lurking doubt how the statue would look, and whether it would not be likely to reflect the reverse of glory upon those who were conspicuous in procuring its erection." New York doesn't lack "men who are at once rich and public-spirited, but there is a lack of men who are willing to [stand accused] of disfiguring the city and bringing it into contempt under pretense of beautifying its harbor." The essential problem, the editors concluded, was that "there was no modern precedent for a statue of these dimensions" and that "whether the statue will be an inexpressive mass or a noble work of art cannot be told until it is seen in the place and at the distance for which it was designed."[19]

The Statue of Liberty, in other words, was too risky a venture, its sculptor too little known in the United States, his motives—and those of his country—unclear. Though the *Times* rejected these American fears and hesitations, it seemed to understand them so well as to suggest that its editors shared them to some extent. Meanwhile, other U.S. publications began to mock the fund-raising committee for its apparent failure to tap the American rich. *Frank Leslie's Illustrated Newspaper* pictured "The 'Statue of Liberty' One Thousand Years Later" and still waiting for her pedestal.[20] In this drawing, she's an ancient, decrepit figure, sitting stooped over on a barren rock. Liberty's tablet rests on her lap, and her torch hangs down, as if she's too weak to hold it up. The cartoon shows a workman patching a crumbling cornerstone, presumably the one destined for the still-unbuilt pedestal. *Life Magazine* featured a similar image on

"The 'Statue of Liberty' One Thousand Years Later" (*Frank Leslie's Illustrated Newspaper*, August 30, 1884).

its cover, portraying the Statue of Liberty "as it will appear by the time the pedestal is finished." Here, the statue looks like a slain vampire about to crumble into dust. Her scrawny arm can barely keep the torch aloft.[21] Another image portrayed Liberty's distressed form ankle-deep in the water, freezing cold, and wondering why there's "no place for the sole of my foot."[22] And yet another broached the populist themes that Pulitzer would later mobilize so successfully. It showed a haughty Liberty pointing disdainfully to Uncle

Sam, who tells her, "Here, you sit down and hold what we have of your Pedestal, while I settle the Committee dissension. Jay Gould thinks we have too much Liberty here now."[23]

What these images have in common, beyond the idea that Liberty has been waiting too long, is the statue's personification as a real human being. She's no longer an inert copper sculpture, an abstract allegory of freedom and enlightenment, but a flesh-and-blood woman with feelings and attitudes like our own. Such personification began shortly after Bartholdi unveiled Liberty's definitive model in 1875 and helps explain why both the French and the American fund-raising campaigns ultimately succeeded. Thanks to a rapidly growing illustrated press, millions of people in France, America, and elsewhere in the world came to know, and identify with, the Statue of Liberty long before the monument went up. Illustrated magazines and newspapers gave her a virtual existence before her actual one and made it difficult for readers to imagine New York Harbor and the world without her. The Statue of Liberty eventually took actual, material form partly because she already existed in the minds and imaginations of people everywhere.

In this dawning age of mass culture, penny papers—read by tens of millions of people—made the Statue of Liberty into a celebrity. Although celebrities surely existed before the birth of the industrialized press in the 1860s, this early mass medium did much to usher in a culture of celebrity whose exemplars enjoyed the ability to shape public perceptions. The more celebrated the virtual Statue of Liberty became, the greater the likelihood that her virtual existence would become a real existence—though without making the virtual statue disappear. Since October 1886, when Bartholdi's monument finally took its place in New York Harbor, its fixed sculptural form has stood alongside its anthropomorphic one, allowing the statue's meanings and uses to multiply and slip beyond anyone's control.

As for Liberty's popularity, nothing worked better than the illusion of bringing her to life. And no one understood this phenomenon better than Pulitzer, whose dramatic intervention ultimately saved the pedestal campaign. In one editorial after another, the publisher spoke of the statue as if it were a human being and, at the time of her inauguration, went so far as to "interview" her about the New York mayoral campaign of 1886. In that campaign, Abram Hewitt of the city's Democratic machine (Tammany Hall) squared off against a young Republican named Theodore Roosevelt and the independent candidate Henry George. Pulitzer was a Democrat, and in his interview Miss Liberty rejected Roosevelt as the representative of big money and George for his dangerous radicalism. She endorsed Hewitt and urged readers to vote for him. The Tammany candidate narrowly defeated George, with the future president a distant third.

Although Pulitzer didn't see the Statue of Liberty as a beacon for immigrants to America, his own background could have made him understand her that way. Austrian-born and half-Jewish, Pulitzer immigrated to the United States in 1863. He fought for the Union army and then settled in Saint Louis, where he went to work for a German-language newspaper and eventually bought two mainstream papers, the *Post* and the *Dispatch*. He merged the two and made the *Post-Dispatch* one of the most influential journals in the West. Pulitzer himself became a prominent businessman and community leader, a young man intent on making his mark. Traveling to New York en route to Europe in May 1883, he heard that Jay Gould, the railroad magnate, wanted to sell the New York *World*, which was losing money every year. Instead of crossing the Atlantic, Pulitzer bought the paper, paying Gould the vast sum of $350,000, the equivalent of $8 million today and far more than it was worth.

Still, in Pulitzer's hands, the *World* quickly erased Gould's losses and became a money-making concern. Pulitzer succeeded in part by dropping the paper's newsstand price to one penny and undercutting his main New York rivals, the *Sun*, *Herald*, and *Tribune*. He then transformed the paper from a stodgy business and high-society journal into a paragon of the sensationalist newspaper style invented forty years earlier by James Gordon Bennett's *New York Herald.* Pulitzer taught his journalists to write sprightly, colorful prose accessible to modestly educated working people, and he gave the *World* a populist, antiestablishment tone. Like Bennett, but especially Moses Millaud, founder of France's *Petit Journal,* Pulitzer focused on lurid crimes, political and financial scandal, and celebrities. He sprinkled illustrations throughout each issue, enlarged the typeface, and employed bold headlines to entice readers and sell papers. Rather than simply report the news, Pulitzer devised ways to create it. He hired Nellie Bly to feign insanity and enter a mental institution suspected of treating poor people inhumanely. Her undercover reporting produced a sensation, making her famous and her boss a powerful New York force. Bly's next stunt was to follow the path Jules Verne had sketched in *Around the World in Eighty Days,* attempting to best his hero's time. En route, she sent telegraphed dispatches, which Pulitzer featured on his front page. When she returned to New York in seventy-two days the *World* bragged, "Father Time Outdone." In his first two years as publisher, Pulitzer increased the *World*'s circulation by a factor of ten, to 153,000. By 1885, his paper was the largest in New York.[24]

The Statue of Liberty had captured his attention right from the start. In 1883, he undertook a brief fund-raising campaign but quickly refocused his interest on the presidential election of 1884. Shamed by Pulitzer's capacity to create a stir, the official fund-raising committee now turned to the New York state and federal governments for help. These efforts, however, succumbed to party politics and to personal animosities associated with them. The New York fund-raisers mostly belonged to the Republican Party, and, unfortunately for them, the governor of New York, Grover Cleveland, was a Democrat. In the spring of 1884, Cleveland vetoed as unconstitutional the state legislature's appropriation of $50,000 for the pedestal. The governor still simmered with grudges left over from the disputed presidential election of 1876, which ultimately went to the Republican candidate, Rutherford B. Hayes, even though his Democratic opponent, Samuel J. Tilden, won the popular vote and initially led in the Electoral College. Cleveland likely felt disinclined to help the pedestal's fund-raising organization, since one of the American Committee's most visible members was the Republican attorney William M. Evarts, who as his party's chief counsel had helped engineer Hayes's electoral victory. Partisan grudges also helped kill $100,000 in federal funds for the pedestal, when a powerful Democratic member of Congress stripped it from a large appropriations bill.[25]

The Democrats' hostility to the official fund-raising committee cooled at the end of 1884, when Cleveland became the first Democrat to win a presidential election since 1856. Pulitzer's *World* had worked hard to elect the New York governor, and with his victory assured the publisher turned his full attention to the Statue of Liberty and its pedestal. At the time of Cleveland's inauguration on March 4, 1885, Pulitzer faced an urgent situation. Bartholdi had officially turned the statue over to the United States the previous July 4, and it was now dismantled and ready for shipment to New York. Bedloe's Island, however, possessed only part of Liberty's foundation, and just a hint of its pedestal.

This time Pulitzer resolved to do everything in his power to raise the money that had eluded the official committee. In a front-page editorial, he announced a plan to collect the missing $100,000 by having his readers send in whatever modest sum they could afford, even if only a nickel or a dime. "We must raise the money! The WORLD is the people's paper, and it now appeals to the people to come forward. . . . Let us not wait for the millionaires to give this money."[26] To attract donations, he promised to publish the name of every contributor, an idea enormously appealing to individuals who would otherwise never see their names in print. In part, Pulitzer's campaign represented yet another journalistic stunt, an effort to create sensational news. But he also appeared to share Bartholdi's moderate republican ideals and to recognize the great populist potential in having ordinary New Yorkers accomplish what the wealthy elite had left undone. "The [pedestal's] corner-stone is a block of the 'finest close-grained granite.' If it is half as 'close-grained' as the churlish millionaires of New York who have manifested their contempt for Liberty and buttoned up their pockets . . . it must be a wonderful specimen."[27]

Pulitzer treated the pedestal campaign as he had the presidential one. He wrote editorials practically every day and ran articles, many on the front page, about the fund-raising effort. The articles featured letters, both invented and real, from the donors. "Please receive from two little boys one dollar for the pedestal," read one. "It is our savings. We give it freely." "Inclosed [*sic*] please find five cents as a poor office boy's mite," announced another. Pulitzer highlighted a fifty-cent donation from a "boy with a salary of $5.00 per month" and two dollars from "a young man of foreign birth" who had "seen enough of monarchical governments to appreciate the blessing of this Republic."[28] The editor, of course, published only a carefully selected portion of the letters he received, so we can have no idea of the full gamut of responses. Still, there is evidence that not all humble Americans endorsed his goals. One Chinese immigrant, writing with the Chinese Exclusion Act of 1882 in mind, declared that the Statue of Liberty offered little freedom to him: "As for the Chinese who are here, are they allowed to go about everywhere free from the insults, abuse, assault, wrongs and injuries from which men of other nationalities are free?"[29]

Pulitzer's populist campaign moved the official fund-raising committee to issue an "Appeal to Patriotism," which took the form of a threat: "If the money is not now forthcoming the statue must return to its donors, to the everlasting disgrace of the American people, or it must go to some other city, to the everlasting dishonor of New York." The *World* greeted this appeal with populist scorn: "Let us, if we can, prevent any syndicate of patriotism among the capitalists. We want the Pedestal built with the dimes of the people, not with the dollars of the rich few."[30]

This is exactly what happened. Contributions to Evarts's American Committee nearly ceased—a sign perhaps that wealthy donors were put off by Pulitzer's rhetoric—while the *World*'s fund-raising effort grew from $2,000 after the first week to $11,600 after the third. Letters continued to pour in, and one included a handwritten verse:

Should Liberty come, any day,
('Tis April, and soon will be May,)
And find not a place in the land
Whereon she could solidly stand,
You would deem it a sin
If you hadn't chipped in.[31]

Although most other New York papers failed to endorse their competitor's campaign, which quadrupled the *World*'s readership and made it (according to Pulitzer) the Western Hemisphere's largest newspaper, journalists from other cities weighed in with their support. As the Ottumwa, Iowa, *Democrat* wrote, "The New York Pedestal Fund has reached $6,000. The Vanderbilt tomb is to cost $200,000. The price of one Vanderbilt is about thirty Liberty Pedestals." Philadelphia's Colonel Forney called Pulitzer "the most eminent citizen of New York," and Bartholdi wrote him to announce, "The colossal Statue of Liberty is ready to be embarked on the Government vessel *Isère*. . . . We hope its arrival will contribute to the completion of the pedestal."[32]

On May 15 Pulitzer's fund had reached $70,000, and on that day the *World* received a $30,000 check from William K. Vanderbilt. It turned out to be a forgery, as Pulitzer gleefully reported two days later. Quarters, dimes, and dollars continued to arrive, and, on August 11, 1885, the *World's* front page showed a triumphant Statue of Liberty waiving an American flag in her torch hand and holding a fistful of dollars in the other. The banner headline announced, "ONE HUNDRED THOUSAND DOLLARS!" And Liberty's pedestal bore the inscription, chiseled by Uncle Sam, "This pedestal to LIBERTY was provided by the voluntary contributions of 120,000 PATRIOTIC CITIZENS of the American Union through the *NEW YORK WORLD*." The inscription was true. More than 121,000 people, many of them farmers, clerks, factory hands, policemen, immigrants, housewives, and children—had sent in a total of $102,000. Thanks to Pulitzer, the pedestal campaign reached its goal; his readers had contributed one-third of the total needed.

This campaign represented a stunning personal success for Pulitzer, a paradigmatic American self-made man, and bore witness to the newfound power of the penny press. In 1885 a media campaign accomplished what an elite group of wealthy and well-connected men could not. No one can know what would have happened had Pulitzer failed to intervene; with a crated Statue of Liberty languishing on Bedloe's Island, Congress may well have put up the remaining $100,000. But it's not impossible that without the *World's* groundbreaking campaign, Liberty would have sat unassembled for years—or even that some other city, Philadelphia perhaps, would have claimed it. Although Bartholdi intended it for New York Harbor, it could have found a place in Fairmount Park or on the banks of the Delaware River, where Phillies and Eagles fans could have seen it from their seats.

FIVE

The Unveiling

With the funding in place, the pedestal began to take shape in the fall of 1885. Before starting on it, workmen had to complete the concrete foundation that would support both the pedestal and the statue itself. To accomplish the task, the chief engineer, General Charles P. Stone, and his head builder, David H. King, Jr., recruited "an army of Italians," as *Leslie's Illustrated Weekly* put it, to mix the cement and mold the foundation's pyramidal structure. The imported Italians resided in a series of rough barracks hastily built on Bedloe's Island, and *Leslie's* drawings show the laborers washing their clothes and themselves in wood basins outdoors. Other sketches placed the workers at rows of dining tables crammed inside the barracks, where they slept on bare wooden bunks. We don't know how much these laborers earned—likely not much—but we can surmise that officials allowed them to remain in the United States.

Leslie's kept a close eye on the construction process, describing the foundation early on as a "huge shapeless bulk crowned with an immense crane." Because the structure "was planted on the highest point of the island," it was "plainly visible from the Battery." A great many New Yorkers found themselves drawn to it, as boatloads of gawkers took the short excursion to see the construction close up.[1] Once the foundation was done, workers laid a massive, six-ton cornerstone of solid granite. A traditional Masonic ceremony followed, with New York Grand Master William A. Brodie presiding. "No other organization," Brodie declared, "has ever done more to promote liberty and to liberate men from their chains of ignorance and tyranny than Freemasonry." A Mason himself, Bartholdi likely agreed, but some critics condemned the Statue of Liberty for its association with Freemasonry, considering it a symbol of paganism. In a box fitted beneath the cornerstone, officials placed the business cards of the dignitaries present, copies of the Declaration of Independence, the Constitution, George Washington's farewell address, the main newspapers of that day, and a poem titled "Liberty Enlightening the World." Included as well were various medals and postage stamps, a portrait of Bartholdi, a list of contributors to the Pedestal Fund, and a coin inscribed with the words of one General Dix: "If any man attempts to haul down the American Flag, shoot him on the spot."[2]

With the cornerstone cemented in, work on the pedestal could proceed. The American Committee had rejected as prohibitively expensive Hunt's original idea to use nothing but pure granite. Instead, General Stone proposed to hang a granite veneer on a core of concrete. A wealthy contractor, King promised to build the project at cost, taking no profit for himself, but the materials he wanted didn't come cheap. King selected the New York region's highest-quality stone: Stony Creek granite carefully mined from Beattie's Quarry on Leete's Island, Connecticut. John Beattie, the Scottish immigrant who owned the quarry, had supplied granite for prominent buildings in Boston and New York as well as for the abutments of the Brooklyn Bridge. Beattie personally recruited the workers and masons for Liberty's pedestal, many from abroad. His people cut each stone individually and then coded the pieces in an effort to keep the sections of a given stone together. Each had its own pattern, and Beattie wanted to maintain their symmetry, thus giving the granite veneer an especially elegant look.[3]

By May 1886, observers could perceive Eiffel's spindly iron skeleton poking up from inside Hunt's granite-faced base. Meanwhile, the statue itself was being unpacked from its two-hundred-odd shipping containers, some crates weighing as much as three tons. As Liberty's skeleton went up, workmen distributed the statue's numbered pieces in a semblance of order around the island—as if to complete the jigsaw puzzle once again. The photographers and sketch artists who documented the process revealed the oddity of an island strewn with gigantic copper pieces. The face, several times taller than any human being, stood propped up in a wooden frame, seemingly watching as builders riveted the pieces of her body together. Liberty's huge toes sat next to a portion of the torch, and journalists commented endlessly on her "titanic tootsies."[4] Towering fingers pointed toward the pedestal and eventually the iron interior, which, when finished in July 1886, looked literally, not just metaphorically, like a skeleton.

The pedestal's girth, together with strong harbor winds, made impractical the kind of scaffolding used in Paris, so one team of workers had to hoist each copper piece of Liberty's skin by ropes and pulleys, while another dangled like rock climbers as they riveted the sections in place. *Leslie's* described the scene: "Workmen are at present moving like industrious ants over the classic draperies and uplifted arm of the mighty figure. They remind one of the Lilliputians swarming over Gulliver in the picturebooks [*sic*]; or . . . like New Jersey mosquitoes attacking a summer boarder."[5] New York artists and photographers, like their Parisian counterparts, seemed fascinated by the headless statue, which looked almost demonic in the countless drawings that showed her fully draped body topped by a skeletal skull. In the end, the Lilliputians had fused the hundreds

Drawing of statue construction on Bedloe's Island showing Liberty headless.

of copper pieces together with more than three hundred thousand rivets, hammered flat to make them all but invisible.

Efforts to illuminate the statue proved inadequate at best; the process of lighting the torch, which involved cutting holes into its base, allowed rainwater to wash in and made the statue vulnerable to deterioration. The dull glow produced from within did nothing for passing ships, though it attracted flocks of birds, whose droppings didn't help. By the last days of October the statue was done, constructed for the second and final time—at least until its toe-to-torch restoration a century later. The Statue of Liberty now belonged, once and for all, to the United States.

Officials scheduled its formal unveiling for October 28, 1886. The Fourth of July would have been a better date—with, as it turned out, better weather as well—but all the delays, exacerbated by misnumbered pieces, edges bent in transit, the lighting fiasco, and myriad other problems, meant that Liberty wasn't ready until the fall. At first it seemed as though President Cleveland, having vetoed state funds for the pedestal, wouldn't come. But in the end, the idea of inaugurating the modern-day Colossus of Rhodes, clearly one of the man-made wonders of the world, proved irresistible. He agreed to preside. His presence turned the unveiling into a major national occasion and began the process of redefining the Statue of Liberty as not just a New York monument but a national one as well.

For the inauguration, French and American dignitaries assembled on Bedloe's Island beneath the gigantic statue. Bartholdi, of course, represented the French, and New Yorkers lionized him as if a latter-day Lafayette. He received the Freedom of the City, much like being honored with the key to a city today, and declared, "The dream of my life is accomplished."[6] Also representing France was Ferdinand de Lesseps, who had begun work on the Panama Canal and hoped to convince a skeptical U.S. government to give its support. (Lesseps's Panama effort ultimately collapsed under the weight of financial scandal and its terrible human costs—twenty-one thousand dead from overwork and disease.) Meanwhile, New York City declared the inauguration a public holiday and staged an elaborate parade with a hundred bands and marching firefighters, policemen, soldiers, national guardsmen, veterans, club members, college students, and local officials. The route was festooned with thousands of French and American flags, and perhaps a million people turned out to watch. Hawkers did a brisk business in Liberty trinkets and souvenirs.

When finally installed, the Statue of Liberty found great favor with the inhabitants of New York. As the *Morning Journal* described the scene: "In every direction extended the crowds up and down Fifth Avenue. House-tops were dense with them. . . . Flags and streamers fluttered heavily in the slight breeze from the roofs and windows of nearly every building. . . . Men climbed up the telegraph poles and . . . every street lamp was surmounted by a small boy . . . to the imminent peril of their lives and to the annoyance of the police."[7] After the parade passed the reviewing stand at Madison Square, invited dignitaries boarded the president's ship, the U.S.S. *Despatch*, which headed a naval parade of some three hundred vessels before docking at Bedloe's Island. The day was cloudy, drizzly, and dark, the statue partially shrouded in the harbor's fog, her face veiled by a huge tricolor flag. But for at least one French reporter, none of that mattered. "I'll never forget," he wrote that afternoon, "the impression of grandiosity, even infinity, that took hold of me when I first glimpsed this eighth wonder of the world!" Liberty loomed like a "gigantic shadow," like "some fantastic apparition of a queen of the seas, emerging all aglow from her liquid domains and advancing, mysterious and veiled, to greet her visitors."[8]

The speeches began in the rain, and they were as dreary as the late-fall sky. Injecting a dose of needed excitement was a miscommunication in which Bartholdi, perched high above in Liberty's torch and unable to hear anything below, released the veil several minutes early—right in the middle of a droning speech by William Evarts, now a U.S. senator. The crowd erupted with joy in seeing Liberty's face, and as if intentionally drowning out the politician's words, the uproar lasted a full fifteen minutes. When quiet finally descended, President Cleveland declared, "We will not forget that Liberty has made here her home, nor shall her chosen altar be neglected."[9]

The day's most significant speech came from Chauncey M. Depew, one of the era's most famous orators and the embodiment of New York City's Republican elite. Depew served as president of the Union League Club, president of the New York Central and Hudson River Railroad, and president of the Yale Alumni Association. His speech paid homage to Bartholdi and to French-American friendship, and referred grandiosely to ancient Greece and Rome, William Tell, Oliver Cromwell, Lexington and Concord, and the fall of the Bastille. He also linked the Statue of Liberty to the violent labor conflict raging in the United States amid the era's extremely difficult conditions for industrial workers.

The 1880s saw nearly ten thousand strikes and lockouts, and in 1886, the year of the Statue of Liberty's inauguration, the strike movement culminated in a "Great Upheaval" in which almost seven hundred thousand workers walked off their jobs. Labor leaders called for a general strike on May 1 of that year, which three hundred thousand workers observed in a vain effort to limit the workday to eight hours. Chicago served as the center of the movement, and, on May 3, police killed four strikers at the McCormick Harvester Company. The next day a protest meeting took place in downtown Chicago's Haymarket Square, and although some anarchists urged violence, labor leaders rejected their demands. The meeting unfolded peacefully until its conclusion, when an unidentified attacker tossed a pipe bomb into the crowd. One policeman died immediately, and in the riot that ensued, for which the forces of order had come well prepared, seven more policemen lost their lives along with four civilians. The authorities arrested eight known anarchists, none of whom they could connect to the bombing, but a court convicted all eight of murder, and four received the death penalty the following year. The Haymarket Eight appealed the verdict, and, just three weeks before the statue's unveiling, members of the group were allowed to address the court. They spoke of liberty and freedom and the lack of both for American workers, forced to toil ten to twelve hours a day even as hourly wages declined. *Harper's Weekly*, which covered the trial extensively, appeared unconvinced by their point of view. The magazine's editors called the guilty verdicts a great service "to liberty in this country" by demonstrating "that liberty does not mean . . . license."[10]

In his speech on Bedloe's Island, Depew echoed *Harper's* themes. For him, the Statue of Liberty meant the "enfranchisement of the individual, the equality of all men before the law and universal suffrage." But it also meant that "the problems of labor and capital, of property and poverty, will work themselves out under the benign influence of enlightened law-making and law-abiding liberty, without the aid of kings and armies, or of anarchists and bombs."[11] That most strikers eschewed violence was, for Depew, beside the point. Strikes themselves infringed on the orderly, "law-abiding" liberty Depew wanted to protect. Union leaders saw liberty differently: not only as the freedom to strike—and the strike itself as a liberation from an employer's top-down authority—but as the emancipation from want at a time when 40 percent of American workers lived below the $500-a-year poverty line and 16 percent were unemployed.[12] Lucy Parsons, the wife of Albert Parsons, one of the convicted four executed in the wake of Haymarket, declared, "Liberty [exists] for the rich, but not for the poor." She called the Haymarket verdicts "a stain upon American liberty."[13]

In the New York mayoral campaign, which reached its final fevered days during the Statue of Liberty's inauguration, Henry George, like Parsons, sought to claim the statue's meaning for those who labored in factories and fields: "'Liberty, Equality, and Fraternity' embodies the aspiration of every workingman in the world today." But during the unveiling ceremony Cleveland joined Depew in recalling Bartholdi and Laboulaye's moderate view of the statue's symbolic intent. "Instead of grasping in her hand the thunderbolts of terror and death, she [the Statue of Liberty] holds aloft the light that illuminates the way to man's enfranchisement." A full-page cartoon in the popular magazine *Puck* reinforced the president's views. It showed the forces of labor—"socialism, anarchism, Georgism [referring to Henry George], boycott, and intolerance"—trying, unsuccessfully, to dismantle the statue. Significantly, Bartholdi's Liberty is rebaptized in this drawing as a fully American "Columbia." Her face has changed completely, looking now like a real woman rather than an allegorical goddess. Instead of the seven-spoked crown, she wears a cap that shows her new American identity as a Columbia hailing from the New World and no longer from the Old.

Although Laboulaye and Bartholdi had intended Liberty in part to symbolize the abolition of slavery, by the time of its dedication African American views of the monument were ambivalent at best. The black-owned *Cleveland Gazette* gave the ceremony in New York Harbor extensive coverage, but it also ran the following editorial: "Shove the Bartholdi statue, torch and all, into the ocean until the 'liberty' of this country is such as to make it possible for an industrious and inoffensive colored man in the South to earn a respectable living for himself and family, without being ku-kluxed[,] perhaps murdered, his daughter and wife outraged, and his property destroyed. The idea of the 'liberty' of this country 'enlightening the world,' or even Patagonia, is ridiculous in the extreme."[14]

The *Cleveland Gazette* withheld this denunciation until a month after the inauguration; on October 28 few editors publicly disagreed with President Cleveland and Depew's point of view. Most African American newspapers avoided the statue's inauguration altogether, allowing silence to stand in for ambivalence or hostility toward a monument to liberty that, as the *Cleveland Gazette* made clear, seemed a slap in the face.[15] It's no mystery why African American commentators were ambivalent at best; the black population suffered especially cruelly during the 1880s and 1890s. In 1883 the U.S. Supreme Court ruled unconstitutional the Civil Rights Act of 1875, which forbade discrimination in trains, hotels, and other public places. To many, this ruling violated the spirit and the letter of the Fourteenth Amendment, which prohibited states from denying basic rights to their residents and granted them equal protection under the law. As Bishop Henry McNeil Turner wrote, "The United States Supreme Court . . . has made the ballot of the black man a parody, his citizenship a nullity and his freedom a burlesque."[16]

Even before the Supreme Court overturned the Civil Rights Act, members of the Ku Klux Klan and other white supremacists began taking the law into their own hands. The Reconstruction period (1865–77) launched an epidemic of lynching that reached its peak in the 1890s. During this decade more than 1,200 black Americans were murdered in acts of vigilante justice—usually hanging but sometimes also torture and mutilation.[17] Although accounts in popular culture have associated lynching mostly with public allegations of the rape or attempted rape of a white woman, in fact two-thirds of all lynching victims had been accused of other crimes, either informally by a local white population or formally by a prosecutor. Many of the accusations were for petty offenses such as verbal abuse or unfair business practices, and all too often the evidence in these cases, as in those supposedly involving murder and rape, was flimsy at best.[18]

As vigilante justice during this time took the lives of more than two black men every week, a series of laws enacted in Southern states undid the new citizenship rights that African Americans had won during Reconstruction. Beginning in the 1870s, when local whites returned to power in the South, one state after the other passed legislation segregating public places—schools, parks, restaurants, restrooms—and assigning lower-quality facilities to African Americans. To ensure that these new rules would remain in place, white politicians enacted "Jim Crow" laws, statutes that, in essence, deprived most blacks of their basic rights—the right to vote, serve on juries, and run for office. In 1896 the famous *Plessy v. Ferguson* Supreme Court ruling affirmed the constitutionality of segregation and, by extension, of the entire Jim Crow system, in arguing that the separation of the races did not necessarily imply the superiority of one over the other. This was, of course, nonsense, as many Americans, black and white, understood. But Jim Crow laws and practices remained firmly in place, and their violation of the most essential American freedoms left a great many African Americans skeptical of the Statue of Liberty's meaning for them.[19]

It didn't help when a white Texas journalist named W. C. Braun wrote that he'd be happy to see Southern blacks flee lynch mobs by moving to New York. If they did, Manhattanites "had better put sheet-iron lingerie on the Statue of Liberty or some morning they would find the old girl with her head mashed in and bearing the marks of sexual violence."[20] Braun's words made the statue a reminder of the oppression, not the liberation, of black men, a reminder of the very attitudes that moved vigilante mobs. W. E. B. DuBois, the distinguished African American writer and activist, vented with playful irony his own negative feelings about the statue in a passage from his *Autobiography*. Describing his 1894 return through New York Harbor from a long European trip, DuBois wrote, "I know not what multitude of emotions surged in the others, but I had to recall that mischievous little French girl whose eyes twinkled as she said: 'Oh, yes, the Statue of Liberty! With its back toward America, and its face toward France!'"[21] Here, the black intellectual turned Bartholdi's intentions upside down. If the Frenchman wanted to commemorate the United States as the homeland of liberty, DuBois, having experienced his country's racist realities firsthand, saw the sculptor's birthplace as the more freedom-loving land.

African American champions of civil rights were reluctant for good reason to stage public demonstrations of dissent; they paid little attention to the Statue of Liberty, even on its inauguration day. Meanwhile, advocates of women's suffrage, mostly white women who hailed from the solid middle class, boldly aimed their own skepticism of the monument into the very heart of the unveiling itself. They sounded a note of dissonance that pierced the symphony of liberal accord and Franco-American amity holding center stage on that rainy afternoon. Members of the Woman Suffrage Association, upset that just two women had been invited to the ceremony on Bedloe's Island, sailed a chartered boat into the harbor. Amid the much more impressive vessels moored nearby, the feminists glided within earshot of the festivities. Together they denounced the hypocrisy of "erecting a Statue of Liberty embodied as a woman in a land where no woman has political liberty."

The suffragists had a point. They might also have noted, as feminist scholars have in recent years, that the French gift of a female image rather than a male one constituted a meaningful choice. It referred to the traditional European politics of marriage in which one monarch donated a sister or daughter to seal a political alliance with another. And it harked back to ancient customs and tribal cultures, which routinely used women as commodities of exchange, sometimes freely given but more often taken and recaptured by force.

If nineteenth-century suffragists found hypocrisy in a female Liberty offered to a country that denied women rights, many others doubtless saw in her the confirmation of prevailing gender roles. Bartholdi had, after all, rejected the revolutionary goddess of liberty for the conservative one, the frankly sexual Marianne of Delacroix's

Liberty Leading the People for the unerotic mother figure he ulti-mately produced. Still, there is nothing weak or demure about his colossal mother of the harbor. Her massive size dwarfed all existing statues of men, and, as constructed, she appears to stride deliber-ately toward the ships in her path. Her powerful arm holds a heavy torch aloft, and she seems to preside, as if a ruler, over the entrance to a great nation-state.

SIX

Huddled Masses

Many histories of the Statue of Liberty end with its unveiling in 1886, adding at most a coda or short epilogue that hastily takes the story to the present. Even the magnificent exhibition catalogue prepared as part of the statue's centennial commemoration devotes only about 50 of its 275 pages to what it calls the "One Hundred Years" of its existence.[1] In many ways, this focus on the conception and creation of the Statue of Liberty makes sense. Although we generally take the monument for granted today, its history reveals just how remarkable its realization was—how improbable the project, how difficult its funding, how uncertain its reception in the United States. It is amazing that the statue ever got built and thus unsurprising that so many books end with the triumph of its inauguration.

Still, there are many reasons to tell the story of the statue's century and a quarter of life. Although its outward appearance has changed little over the years, despite an elaborate—and much needed—structural refreshment in the 1980s, the statue's meaning has evolved markedly. It has meant so many different things to so many different people that its very symbolic malleability demands nearly as much attention as its creation. To successful businessmen it meant free enterprise and the order and discipline imposed by laws intended to apply equally to everyone. To labor leaders, liberty meant the right to strike for better wages and working conditions, and the freedom from want. For advocates of women's suffrage, liberty meant that women should be as free politically as men. For African Americans living under the segregation, inequality, and disenfranchisement of Jim Crow laws, the statue's original abolitionist message had long been forgotten. The monument now appeared to them bitterly ironic, as representing a freedom once promised and now denied.

As labor conflict sharpened in the late nineteenth century, and women and blacks chafed against restrictive laws and customs, Bartholdi's monument began to lose its luster as a beacon of liberty. It now became central to a new controversy that raged over the huge number of foreigners immigrating to the United States. More often than not—at least in the early years—the Statue of Liberty stood as a symbol of opposition to immigration rather than of welcome to the "huddled masses yearning to breathe free."

From the end of the Civil War to the close of the nineteenth century, the United States transformed itself from a society grounded economically in agriculture and small-scale manufacturing to one built on mechanization, advanced technology, and large-scale corporations. The workshop increasingly gave way to the factory, which needed a huge labor force and energy supplied by coal, whose extraction also required a great many workers. Many of the new industrial tasks demanded only a minimum of skill and education, which meant that almost any able-bodied person could perform it. But in 1865, the U.S. population was still too sparse to provide all the bodies needed, and besides, many native-born workers, having been trained in a particular skill, resisted the new factory and mining jobs. They were accustomed to small workshops and considerable independence and showed little appetite for routinized labor. In the last decades of the century, many U.S.-born workers had to take such jobs, but American industry expanded so rapidly that employers turned en masse to immigrant labor. Word of work spread quickly to southern and eastern Europe, Russia, and China, where members of minority religious and ethnic groups, suffering from unemployment and oppressive regimes, sought opportunity in the New World.

By the 1880s, what had been a quickening stream of immigrants now became a flood. Between 1880 and 1900, the number of newcomers averaged nearly a half-million a year, compared to an annual average of just 125,000 during the four decades before the Civil War. From January to December 1905, more than a million immigrants arrived, the most in any single year to date. But newcomers smashed that record in 1907, when almost 1.3 million foreigners entered the country. No one knows exactly how many immigrants came, but economic historians estimate the total for the period 1865–1900 at 13.3 million, a number roughly equaled between 1900 and 1914. Close to six million more arrived between 1914 and 1930.[2] Because about one-third of the migrants returned to their native lands, the actual number of permanent new Americans between 1865 and 1930 might have reached twenty-two million. Although some states restricted immigration, the federal government did nothing to discourage the influx. The main exception was the Chinese, who found themselves excluded in 1882 even though they represented a tiny portion of the total. As a result of this relative open door policy, the character of the American population changed dramatically between 1880 and 1914. Until 1881, 86 percent of the country's voluntary immigrants had come from the British Isles, Scandinavia, and German-speaking lands; most quickly blended into a white American population composed mainly of people like them. Irish Catholics, who came in large numbers, constituted an exception, but many "Irish" immigrants were actually Scots-Irish, whose

Protestantism enabled them to fit in almost everywhere they set-tled.[3] After 1881, northern European immigration gave way to new-comers from southern, central and eastern Europe, who between 1894 and 1914 constituted almost 70 percent of those moving to the United States.[4] For the most part, these immigrants, many of them Catholics and Jews, speaking languages unknown in the New World, seemed "foreign"—distinctly different from those already in this country.

A large percentage of the people who poured in from Italy, Po-land, Austria, Greece, Russia, and an array of other places found unskilled jobs. Already by 1870, one of every three industrial work-ers had recently immigrated to the United States, and this propor-tion would hold steady for the next fifty years.[5] With the size of the industrial workforce growing rapidly, the absolute number of im-migrants within it became many millions strong. Since the indus-trial transformation of the United States was both the cause and result of immigration on a mass scale, industrial labor itself now ap-peared foreign. As a Chicago minister put it in 1887, "Not every foreigner is a workingman [but] it may be that every workingman is a foreigner."[6] The clergyman, of course, exaggerated the overall situation, but perhaps not in his native city. In the late nineteenth century, the majority of Chicago's inhabitants were immigrants or the children of immigrants. Since the growing number of white-collar managerial jobs mostly went to the native-born, now identi-fied as the "real Americans," the widening divide between managers and workers, middle class and working class, capital and labor, took on an ethnic, even racialized, hue. Owners and managers were "white," and workers were "dark"—whether originally from Italy or eastern Europe, whether Catholics or Jews. And since working people tended to congregate in particular urban neighborhoods, seeking low-cost (and usually low-quality) housing on the same streets as people like them, city dwellers sorted themselves into enclaves organized by ethnicity and race: Little Italy, Chinatown, the (Jewish) Lower East Side in New York; Greektown and the Polish Triangle in Chicago; Black Bottom in Detroit.

Given these patterns of employment and residence, social divisions in America of the Gilded Age turned not solely on class or ethnicity, but also on the perceived split between "American" and "foreign." When the economic difficulties of the 1870s and '80s produced a torrent of strikes, some involving violence, so-called foreign agitators took the blame. The *New York Times* described these agitators in particularly graphic terms: "roughs, hoodlums, rioters . . . thieves, blacklegs, looters, communists, rabble, labor-reform agitators, dangerous class of people, gangs, tramps, drunken sectionmen, law breakers . . . ruffians, loafers, bullies, vagabonds, cowardly mob, bands of worthless fellows, incendiaries, enemies of society . . . malcontents . . . loud-mouthed orators, rapscallions, brigands, robbers, riffraff, terrible felons, idiots."[7] Thanks to immigration, the United States now seemed at the mercy of alien forces, of foreigners who sought to bring the country to its knees.

The Statue of Liberty became associated with these newcomers by default rather than design. The nature of steamship routes and port facilities on the East Coast meant that the vast wave of immigration that rose in the 1880s mostly headed for New York. Since 1855, European migrants had landed at Castle Garden (or Castle Clinton), a facility operated by the state of New York and located on Manhattan's southern tip. Castle Garden was notorious for abusing newcomers and failing to protect them from the army of pimps, confidence men, contract-labor "padrones," and boardinghouse runners hoping to take their money. In March 1890, Secretary of the Treasury William Windom announced that the U.S. government would assume control of the immigration process. He intended both to shield the newcomers and to limit their number—in large part by excluding people deemed unfit to reside in the United States. Windom charged that New York state officials had allowed in too many people with "contagious and destructive diseases" and too many troublemakers "inimical to our social and political institutions." In other words, New York City, where most Europeans now entered the country, had not been attentive enough either to the rising tide of immigration or to the change "in the character of many of the immigrants, who do not readily assimilate with our people, and are not in sympathy with our institutions."[8] The southern and eastern Europeans just didn't fit in, Windom claimed, and many supposedly ended up in asylums and jails and in jobs once held by native-born workers.

Windom's idea was to quarantine newcomers offshore, where undesirables would pose no threat and where they all would undergo a rigorous examination. He chose for this purpose Bedloe's Island and proposed to erect an immigration processing center next to the Statue of Liberty. If Windom associated the new monument with immigration, and it isn't clear he did, it was to symbolize the exclusion, not the welcome, of Europe's "huddled masses." Bartholdi, for his part, had never linked the statue with immigration, and he immediately condemned Windom's plans for Bedloe's Island as "monstrous." His statue represented orderly American liberty, not Europe's underclass. Still, Windom's proposal, and the harsh reactions it evoked, had the effect, likely unintended, of connecting the flood of immigration to the Statue of Liberty. But the connection established in 1890 contradicts what we generally take to be the relationship between the two. A series of widely circulated political cartoons, editorial commentaries, and even verses by leading poets portrayed the Statue of Liberty as the victim of the new immigration and the symbol of the mounting hostility to it—not the beacon welcoming newcomers to our shores.

"European garbage ships" (*Judge*, March 22, 1890).

That Windom appears as the villain in what may have been the most influential of these late-century cartoons is ironic, because he shared the cartoonists' anti-immigrant views. Shortly after the secretary's announcement about Bedloe's Island, *Judge* chimed in with a pair of nasty cartoons, one on the front cover and one on the back.[9] The first shows a troubled-looking Liberty hiking her robes to avoid touching the ragged immigrants shoveled from "European garbage ships" and dumped at her feet. The caption calls Bedloe's Island

"The Proposed Emigrant Dumping Site" and has the statue declare: "Mr. Windom, if you are going to make this island a garbage heap, I am going back to France." The second image, captioned "The Future Emigrant Lodging House: A Suggestion to Secretary Windom," turns the statue into a squalid tenement building housing anarchists, "Polaks," Germans, Irish, and other undesirables. A rusty fire escape hangs from the blemished monument, as do the emblems of dissolute foreign life: beer saloon, laundry, and Irish shanty. A hammock like the ones used in steerage class, the dank hold where most immigrants huddled en route to the U.S., hangs between two of Liberty's spokes.[10]

Cartoons in *Judge*'s main competitor, *Puck*, hit even harder. The magazine's Louis Dalrymple pictured a toppled statue, its arm severed, lying atop a chaos of ramshackle buildings, including an "immigrant lodging house" and "baggage express." The setting doubles as a junkyard, with Liberty advertised "for sale as old metal." What's left of her foundation sports the sign "Immigrants Land Here!" Seedy, indistinct figures carrying oversized duffle bags surround the broken-down statue, whose torch points upward, and where we see two figures presiding over the scene: a fat-cat businessman perched on a Doric-columned bank and, above him, a cowboy-garbed Boss Platt representing New York State's formidable Republican machine. The coils of Platt's whip spell out "bossism." The meaning of both figures is clear: money and politics rule, and it's to bolster that rule that so many undesirables have been invited in. The new rabble will work cheaply for the country's moneyed interests, and their eventual votes will feed Platt's statewide machine.[11]

In yet another influential cartoon, the Statue of Liberty holds her nose as she tramps through the muck of immigration, the "Dregs of Europe," that soils Bedloe's Island. Liberty holds a bottle of carbolic acid, the strongest antiseptic known at the time. She doubtless intends to sanitize the island of the disease-ridden European rabble

"Boss Platt's latest outrage" (*Puck*, March 19, 1890).

washed up on its shore.[12] Faced with images such as these, U.S. officials had no choice but to abandon Bedloe's Island as its reception center; they ultimately settled on Ellis Island, next door.[13]

Doing so may have calmed some opponents of open-door immigration, but not Thomas Bailey Aldrich, editor of the influential

"Dregs of Europe" (*Evening Telegram*, September 10, 1892).

Atlantic Monthly and one of the country's best-known poets. In 1892 Aldrich wrote a verse that he characterized to a friend as a "protest against America becoming a cesspool of Europe."[14] Titled "Unguarded Gates," the poem condemns the "wild, motley throng" pouring in, those "bringing with them unknown gods and rites,/ Those, tiger passions, here to stretch their claws." Turning to Bartholdi's monument, the poet asks, "O Liberty, white Goddess! Is it well/to leave the gates unguarded?" Is it well, that is, for her to let her dark counterparts through, these strangers with "accents of

menace alien to our air,/Voices that once the Tower of Babel knew!"
For Aldrich, who made "Unguarded Gates" the title poem of a book
he published in 1895, the ultimate danger was the same one that
had brought the fall of Rome: "The thronging Goth and Vandal
trampled Rome,/And where the temples of the Caesars stood/The
lean wolf unmolested made her lair." As if the poem wasn't clear
enough, Aldrich explained to his friend, "I believe in America for
Americans."[15]

These sentiments, coming as they did from a paragon of the
United States' cultural elite, hardly represented a fringe protest or
isolated voice; they came straight from the American establishment
and formed much of the context in which the federal government
opened its immigration center on Ellis Island in 1892. Still, such
protests did little to slow the influx of Europeans; the demand for
labor and Washington's willingness to admit newcomers kept the
gates open until after the First World War. During the heyday of
Ellis Island, from the 1890s until the Immigration [exclusion] Act
of 1924, more than twelve million immigrants passed through the
facility. The overall number entering the country in New York ex-
ceeded this figure, but only those who traveled third class or steerage had to go to Ellis Island. Immigrants who could afford first- or
second-class accommodations received a quick onboard inspection
followed by an invitation to enter the country directly from the
dock, whether in Manhattan, Brooklyn, or Hoboken. The rest were
unloaded onto ferries and shuttled offshore to the immigration-
processing center.

On arrival, laden with all their worldly possessions, the newcomers had numbered tags pinned to their chests and then faced a battery of doctors from the United States Public Health Service. The
doctors examined them for contagious diseases, physical deformi-
ties, mental disabilities, breathing problems, infections, and hearing
disorders, any of which might make them ineligible to enter the

country. The exams were cursory, consisting largely of what was called the "medical gaze," a quick once-over that lasted between six and forty seconds. Most immigrants passed the medical exam, after which they had to respond to a list of twenty-nine questions: "Who paid for your ship's fare?" "What kind of work can you do?" "Can you read and write?" "How much money do you have?" "Show it to me!" More than a few found themselves bilked of their meager resources, but the overwhelming majority received landing cards that admitted them to the United States. The process generally took less than a day.[16]

While traveling through the Narrows and then back by ferry to Ellis Island, immigrants found themselves constantly in the presence of the Statue of Liberty. Many had doubtless heard of the colossal sculpture before leaving for America, but steerage passengers may not have seen it until released from their airless and windowless hold and onto the ferry bound for the immigration reception center. From there, they could see Liberty at last; her overwhelming presence confirmed that they had finally arrived. The misery of the two-week crossing, a voyage plagued by inedible food, poor sanitation, bad smells, and lack of privacy, now belonged to the past. Open-air ferryboats seemed to take them to the statue itself, and they doubtless hoped to enjoy the freedom and opportunity for which she stood so tall.

Many of those who glimpsed the Statue of Liberty for the first time recorded (or remembered later) what they felt. "Seeing the Statue of Liberty," wrote Arnold Weiss, "was the greatest thing I've ever seen . . . I said to myself, 'Gee, we're in America. Now I can go out in the streets and pick up gold.'" Sarah Asher, arriving from Russia, told an interviewer that she had gotten up at five a.m. and joined her fellow passengers on deck. "The sunshine started, and what do we see? The Statue of Liberty! Well, she was beautiful with the early morning light. Everybody was crying. The whole boat bent toward her . . . and everybody was crying." From one boat to the next, newcomers shed tears of joy. As Mela Neisner Lindsay and her family emerged from the "deep well of steerage into the daylight of a new world," many around them "wept for joy," while others "sang songs of praise in strange tongues" and still others "remained silent, their eyes glistening with fierce hope." For immigrants young and old, the sight of the Statue of Liberty glistening in the harbor evoked feelings of reverence and awe, and to many the green goddess seemed almost divine. "Slowly the ship glides into the harbor," wrote Edward Steiner, "and when it passes under the shadow of the Statue of Liberty, the silence is broken, and a thousand hands are outstretched in a greeting to this new divinity to whose keeping they now entrust themselves. 'Oh Papa,' cried one young girl, 'the goddess has waded into the water to meet us!'"[17]

If immigrants associated the Statue of Liberty with freedom and hope, a great many American editorialists, cartoonists, and politicians continued to use her image to express hostility to the unwashed foreigners they saw as making their country an unrecognizable, perhaps dangerous, place. Still, it helped to physically separate the immigration reception center from the Statue of Liberty, even if the two stood on adjacent islands. And by 1900, as a new period of prosperity ended the strike waves and political violence of the previous decades, public expressions of fear and hostility toward immigrants subsided. The country now seemed capable of integrating the newcomers, and immigration receded for a time as a commanding political issue.

After the turn of the century, a number of once-penniless newcomers who achieved a measure of success began to see the Statue of Liberty as an emblem of their good fortune. In 1902, a Russian immigrant named William H. Flattau erected a fifty-five-foot replica of the statue on the roof of his otherwise nondescript warehouse on

West Sixty-fourth Street. Intent on accuracy, he sent workmen to Bedloe's Island, where they took measurements of Bartholdi's monument and then built a three-foot model, which despite their efforts had the face and a few other details wrong. Flattau then sent the model to an Ohio foundry, which built the fifty-five-foot facsimile in thirty-five separate sections of quarter-inch steel. After riveting them together atop his warehouse, Flattau endowed his masterpiece with a lighted torch visible a mile away, an internal staircase, and windows onto the city from the statue's head. In 1912 a storm destroyed the torch, and Flattau closed his Liberty to visitors, but it remained a neighborhood attraction until new tenement buildings blocked it from view. The replica became visible again in the early 1960s when developers cleared the area to make way for Lincoln Center. Flattau's copy, the largest of all the Liberty replicas, survived the process, and it now stands in a parking lot behind the Brooklyn Museum.[18]

Israel Zangwill, another immigrant of eastern European origin (though born in London), celebrated the Statue of Liberty in his play *The Melting Pot*. First performed in 1908, Zangwill's drama is an ode to cultural assimilation, intermarriage, and harmony across ethnic and religious divides. The play's title would long represent the view of Americanization as a successful melding of cultures. Under the statue's shadow, Zangwill's hero, David Quixano, declares, "Celt and Latin Slav and Teuton Greek and Syrian black and yellow . . . Jew and Gentile . . . East and West and North and South . . . the crescent and the cross" can blend together and live in peace. Although overly optimistic, the play nonetheless expressed the newfound tolerance of the early twentieth century. *The Melting Pot* attracted enthusiastic audiences, and President Theodore Roosevelt made a point of attending its premier in Washington, D.C. The Statue of Liberty appears throughout, and at one point David proclaims, "The same great torch of liberty which threw its light across all the broad seas and lands into my little garret in Russia is shining also for all those other weeping millions of Europe." Despite a measure of public interest in Zangwill's play, editorialists and critics tended to reject the positive connection between immigration and the Statue of Liberty. A. B. Walkley of the *New York Times* labeled "romantic claptrap" the "rhapsodising [*sic*] over crucibles [of assimilation] and statues of Liberty."[19]

Such an attitude helps explain why hardly anyone took notice when in 1903 Emma Lazarus's "The New Colossus" was inscribed on a bronze tablet and placed inside the entrance to the Statue of Liberty. The statue hadn't yet become the tourist attraction it would later be, and her poem attracted no more interest in 1903 than when she had written it twenty years earlier.[20] Even Lazarus herself hadn't always been sensitive to the plight of immigrants to the United States or to the long-standing persecution of the European Jews who represented a growing portion of these newcomers. As a member of a wealthy and well-established Sephardic Jewish family, Lazarus had led a comfortable, sheltered life, writing tranquilly in her family's well-appointed home.

Lazarus's distinguished writing career began at age sixteen with a short book of precocious literary works, mostly poems and translations, none of which revealed any political or social commitments. A few years later she began a long-term correspondence with Ralph Waldo Emerson: he became her most important reader and critic, and she his admiring disciple. Lazarus quickly published another book of poetry and then a novel, *Alide*. These works took her beyond Emerson and transcendentalism and earned her admiration from Ivan Turgenev, John Burroughs, and Walt Whitman, among others. Although she had joined the ranks of noted Americans writers, she wasn't recognized as a Jewish writer until the final years of her tragically short life. Save for one early poem ("In the Jewish Synagogue at Newport," 1867) and an essay on Heinrich Heine, the

German Jewish poet who converted to Christianity (1881), her published work expressed little interest in Jewish life or in her own Jewish identity. Lazarus never disguised her Jewishness and sometimes seemed to revel in her religious difference, but she didn't frequent the synagogue and, like her parents, moved easily in New York's elite Christian society.[21]

Lazarus's relative indifference to Judaism began to change in the late 1870s, when a series of anti-Semitic incidents in and around New York piqued her anger and moved her to express ardently and openly a Jewish pride that she had harbored all along. She went even further in the early 1880s when word of Russia's bloody anti-Jewish pogroms reached the United States. In response to these tragic events, Lazarus's delicate poems and learned literary criticism gave way to sharp polemics against anti-immigrant writers and to lucid essays about America's humanitarian responsibilities. She began to write regularly for the weekly magazine *The American Hebrew* and published several poems with fervently Jewish themes. Lazarus collected those poems in a book titled *Songs of a Semite* and penned a series of essays, *Epistle to the Hebrews* (1882–83), that took up questions of Jewish history and identity while urging eastern European Jews to emigrate to Palestine. These new writings revealed a passion largely absent from her earlier ones, an emotional fire sparked by the anti-Semitic violence of the Russian pogroms. Lazarus also drew inspiration from developments closer to home, especially the juxtaposition of wealth and poverty she saw around her in New York. She reacted to poverty as if seeing it for the first time and felt its effects both on a human, emotional level and through the prism of political ideas advanced by the American radical Henry George.[22]

A popular writer and speaker in the 1880s and 1890s, George advocated high taxes on rental property and moderate imposts on forms of capital he considered productive. He believed in government ownership of "natural monopolies" like telegraph and telephone companies and wrote extensively about the evils of poverty. The latter aroused Lazarus's interest as she began to spend time with Jewish refugees crowded into a squalid immigration holding pen on Wards Island in the East River. There she discovered firsthand the plight of the displaced, of those who had fled from terror and poverty in their home countries and who faced suspicion, even deportation, when they landed in New York. As Lazarus deepened her identification with these Jewish immigrants, she deepened her own self-identification as a Jew. When asked to contribute to Bartholdi's artistic fund-raiser of 1883, Lazarus found herself swayed by the argument that she should "think of that Goddess standing on her pedestal down yonder in the bay, and holding her torch out to those Russian refugees of yours you are so fond of visiting on Ward's Island."[23] Those visits changed her life and inspired her best-known poem, the one eventually grafted to the Statue of Liberty's base.

Although most commentators failed to notice "The New Colossus" when Lazarus originally presented it, the great American poet James Russell Lowell recognized the sonnet's strengths. Lowell wrote Lazarus that her work "gives its subject a *raison d'être* which it wanted before, quite as much as it wants a pedestal." Lowell also complimented Lazarus for "saying admirably just the right word to be said, an achievement more arduous than that of the sculptor." The poet added, though he perhaps didn't need to, "I liked your sonnet about the Statue . . . much better than I like the Statue itself."[24] Although Lowell overestimated the poet's labor relative to the sculptor's, he nonetheless put his finger on precisely what Lazarus contributed to the monument. Through the words of her sonnet, she gave the Statue of Liberty a voice ("just the right word") and granted it the use of the pronoun "I." In doing so, Lazarus breathed a poetic life into Liberty's lifeless form: "'Keep, ancient lands, your storied pomp,' cries she. . . . 'Give me your tired, your poor . . . I lift my lamp beside the golden door.'"[25]

Twenty years later, Israel Zangwill echoed Lowell's sentiments, and a few other "ethnic" writers connected the statue to a positive, hopeful view of immigration. But such views remained in the minority. Although most of O. Henry's stories enjoyed enormous popularity at the turn of the century, his piece about the Statue of Liberty, "The Lady Higher Up," didn't rank among that group. The story, likely written the same year workmen affixed "The New Colossus" to Liberty's base, called the statue a "heroic matron whose duty it is to offer a cast-ironical welcome to the oppressed of other lands." Like Lazarus, O. Henry gave Liberty voice, but he had her speak in Irish brogue: "I was made by a Dago and presented to the American people on behalf of the French Government for the purpose of welcomin' Irish immigrants into the Dutch city of New York. 'Tis that I've been doing night and day since I was erected." Sometimes O. Henry's Liberty is "weary of the gang of immigrants I'm supposed to light up," but "'tis me job to extend aloft the torch of Liberty to welcome all them that survive the kicks that the steerage stewards give 'em while landin'. Sure 'tis a great country ye can come to for $8.50, and the doctor waitin' to send ye back home free if he sees yer eyes red from cryin' for it."[26]

Again, such positive impressions failed to resonate very far—at least not until the First World War, when propagandists used the Statue of Liberty to rally newcomers to the American cause and against the very countries from which many of the immigrants had come. But the postwar U.S. isolationism and the "Red Scare" of the late teens and early '20s once again turned pundits and politicians against the foreigners in their midst, against the immigrants said to import Bolshevism, atheism, and political violence into a threatened United States. Now, as in the 1880s and '90s, cartoonists portrayed Liberty as menaced by the alien evildoers surging across our borders. A famous drawing of 1919 shows a "European anarchist" crouched behind the statue while holding a dagger in one hand and a bomb in

"Come unto me, ye opprest!" (*Literary Digest*, July 5, 1919).

the other. The cartoon's ironic caption reads, "Come unto me, ye opprest!"[27] In another widely circulated drawing, the ocean washes "war" in the form of immigrant humanity onto America's peaceful shores.[28] Such images stood out as cause and symptom of a renewed public hostility to impoverished aliens, and they helped encourage a majority in Congress to close the door to immigration. The Immigration Act of 1924 barred virtually all Asians and restricted the number of immigrants from eastern, central, and southern Europe to a trickle. Between 1910 and 1920, about two hundred thousand

Italians immigrated to the U.S. every year; after 1924, Italian new-comers dropped to four thousand. Meanwhile, the new law set the quota for Germany, America's enemy in 1918, at over fifty-seven thousand. Interestingly, the act established no limits on immigration from Latin America. The problem, so officials believed, stemmed from Italy, Russia, Poland, and other "dangerous" southern and eastern European lands.[29]

Not surprisingly, many of those whose presence had inspired the new law turned against the Statue of Liberty or saw it as unequal to the promise of hope and freedom it was supposed to represent. In 1917 the labor organizer Giuseppe Iannarelli declared, "When the Italians enter this country they see the Statue of Liberty and they breathe freely thinking to themselves that they have at last left the autocratic government and are in the land of the free. Shortly after their arrival they realize their mistake."[30] Carlo Tresca, another left-winger of European origins, echoed these views:

> When the ship which transported us to America passed before the historic, colossal Statue of Liberty there was a joyous rush to the side; all eyes were fixed on that torch of light . . . symbolizing the most dear of human aspirations, *La Liberta*, to see if there was a heart within [the statue] which beat for all of the political refugees, for all of the slaves of capital, for the disinherited of the world. . . . Now I am disillusioned. . . . Perhaps I will pass again, still a pilgrim of the faith, before that statue. Like so many of my comrades—perhaps I will be DEPORTED before these vibrant pages will be read by the Italian workers who suffer, aspire, struggle. Oh, that torch will no longer shine the light it did![31]

If such voices lamented the statue's failure to live up to its ideals—and these constituted the majority of writers disillusioned by the Red Scare and immigration restrictions—some portrayed the statue as symbol of a deep-rooted American evil. The anarchist Luigi Galleani described Lady Liberty as "this monstrous collossus [*sic*], this republic of the heart of anthracite, with the forehead of ice, with the goiterous throat; this statue of cretinism . . . whose hands are armed with a whip, from whose lips are suspended a knife and a revolver."[32]

Not until the 1930s, when the number of newcomers to the United States dropped to almost nothing, did the American public at large come to see the Statue of Liberty as the symbol of immigration and to regard that symbolism in a largely positive light. The politics and policies of the New Deal created the context for this shift in meaning, but it was mostly former immigrants who did the actual cultural work. The Roosevelt administration discouraged the harsh attacks on labor unions characteristic of the previous decade, and since it faced fierce attacks from the right, it tried to soothe tensions between liberals and radicals on the left. But mostly the administration tried to unify a distressed population as much as possible, and that meant fostering more favorable attitudes toward the large number of recent immigrants who now belonged to American society. The journalist Louis Adamic, an immigrant from Slovenia, became central to this effort as he campaigned to persuade teachers to emphasize the important contributions immigrants had made to U.S. history and to present the Statue of Liberty as the symbol of America's welcome to them.[33] He collected testimonies from former immigrants, many of whom spoke or wrote glowingly of their first encounter with the Statue of Liberty, and touted Emma Lazarus's long-neglected poem as holding the key to the statue's meaning. His ultimate goal was "an intellectual-emotional synthesis of the old and new America; of the Mayflower and the steerage . . . of the Liberty Bell and the Statue of Liberty."[34]

Roosevelt tried to do something similar during the celebration of Liberty's fiftieth anniversary in 1936. Standing on Bedloe's Island, with the monument looming behind him, FDR sought to bring Americans together by emphasizing the immigrants' contributions to the country. "By their effort and devotion," the president said, "they made the New World's freedom safer, richer, more far-reaching, more capable of growth." With these comments, he rejected the polarizing, anti-immigrant rhetoric of earlier decades and characterized the newcomers not as alien to American society but as central to it. Still, he relegated immigration to the past, as if that part of American history had ended for good. "We have within our shores today the materials out of which we shall continue to build an ever better home for liberty."[35] The United States, in other words, needed no more newcomers; the door to them would remain essentially closed. Roosevelt's solution to the "immigration question" was thus a compromise. Those already here would be embraced as Americans like any others, but the government saw no need to invite new ones in.

Given the Nazi seizure of power in Germany and the persecution of European Jews, Roosevelt's compromise seemed callous at best to a growing number of American commentators, not all of them Jews. Under Hitler, European Jewry's plight now appeared considerably worse than in the 1880s and 1890s, and sympathy for this group spilled over onto other potential immigrants as well. In this context Lazarus's poem took on new meaning, and it seemed especially important to portray the Statue of Liberty as the poet's "Mother of Exiles," the powerful symbol whose "beacon-hand glows worldwide welcome." Now, on the eve of World War II, an army of writers and artists transformed the statue into an internationally recognized symbol not just of immigrants and immigration but of the great American "golden door," the charmed portal through which the United States welcomes "your tired, your poor,/Your huddled masses yearning to breathe free."

As Emma Lazarus became a household word, artists helped erase most negative connotations from the Statue of Liberty. Ida Abelman's lithograph *My Father Reminisces* (1937) featured a luminous Statue of Liberty presiding over the symbols of immigrant life—for women as well as men: urban ghetto, sweatshop, sewing machine, strike, boss, and union.[36] Meanwhile, Edward Corsi, an immigrant from Italy in 1907 (and later a commissioner of Ellis Island) called the Statue of Liberty "this symbol of America—this enormous expression of . . . the inner meaning of [our] new country."

These prewar developments did much to root Liberty in Americans' consciousness as the expression of a national openness and generosity. After the war, when Ellis Island closed and immigration ceased to be a factor in American life, the Statue of Liberty flowered as a quintessential symbol of the United States, a symbol more important than Uncle Sam or the bald eagle and beginning to rival the Liberty Bell.[37] With the flood of immigrants apparently dammed for good, there were precious few foreigners in our midst; almost everyone could claim to be fully American and, for that reason, the memory of immigration could bask in a nostalgic glow. The violent controversies, nativism, and xenophobia of the early years had subsided, leaving the Statue of Liberty as an icon of American consensus, of the widespread belief that the U.S. motto, E Pluribus Unum—from many, one—had come true.

This consensus was not destined to last.

SEVEN

From Neglect to Commemoration

After New York's exuberant celebration of its new Statue of Liberty in 1886, interest in the monument remained strong as long as immigration evoked controversy. When the controversy died down in the early 1900s, attention to the statue waned as well. Tourists did not yet frequent Bedloe's Island in large numbers, and New Yorkers tended to look inward and away from the waterways that surrounded them.

Between Liberty's dedication in 1886 and its torch-to-toe restoration of the 1980s, Washington largely ignored the monument, whose inner structure and copper skin inevitably deteriorated for want of regular maintenance. The notable exceptions were the Progressive and New Deal eras, when the two Roosevelt administrations agreed to devote some public funds to the statue's upkeep. Even the massive restoration project completed in time for the centennial celebration of 1986 had no government support; the funding came entirely from private sources. If the Statue of Liberty has become one of the greatest symbols of the United States, it is because American people have made it so.

After accepting the Statue of Liberty and inaugurating the monument in 1886, the U.S. government didn't exactly know what to do with it. One of its functions was to serve as a lighthouse, and as such, officials assigned it to the national Light-House Board. But the United States Army also exercised jurisdiction over the monument, because it controlled the little-used military installation, Fort Hood, whose buildings still occupied Bedloe's Island. And finally, the American Committee, the private organization that had lobbied for the statue and raised funds for the pedestal, operated the ferryboats that shuttled between Manhattan and the statue. Each of these entities thought the others should take responsibility for the statue's maintenance, which meant, of course, that none of them did. The result was a chaotic site unaccommodating to visitors and a decaying monument. "Inside and out," wrote the commandant of Fort Hood, "the Statue of Liberty . . . is a distinct disgrace to our country."[1] Echoing the military man, Pulitzer's *World* declared, "The National Government has been shamefully indifferent to the great monument of liberty from the first." Pulitzer had editorialized against locating the immigration reception center on Bedloe's Island—he wanted to keep Liberty and its surroundings "pure"—and now his paper pressured the government to make the site "a pleasure ground for the people."

Despite the editor's pleas, Washington remained supremely indifferent to the statue's fate. In 1890, the Senate rejected a bill to make Bedloe's Island a public park, fearing the "dangerous precedent" of dispensing federal money for the benefit of a single city. After the turn of the century, the statue's situation improved marginally as Progressive-era presidents advocated a more activist government. Warning that the Statue of Liberty would collapse without needed repairs, the Theodore Roosevelt administration got Congress to appropriate a modest sum ($62,800) for the statue's maintenance.

Its interior received a new coat of paint, the pedestal a new granite facing, the island itself a new wharf. There was even enough money to install an elevator to the top of the pedestal.

But the government lacked the resources to fulfill its main objective: the effort to give the statue a powerful source of light. Liberty would spend her first thirty years of life as a beacon largely devoid of illumination, a lighthouse too dim to guide any ships. Once again, the *World* stepped in. In 1915 the paper gave the U.S. War Department a plan to brighten the torch and install floodlights around the statue's base. The newspaper promised to raise $30,000 in donations if the government would agree to match that amount. Congress accepted the arrangement, and the newspaper proved true to its word. In December 1916 President Woodrow Wilson flipped a switch to dramatic effect: suddenly the statue glowed in a warm golden light.

Now New Yorkers could see the Statue of Liberty at night. Such new visibility doubtless helped Liberty become a protected national monument according to the terms of the 1906 Antiquities Act, a status that President Calvin Coolidge confirmed in 1924. But the Progressive era had passed, and Coolidge didn't bestow any new funding on a structure once again needing repair. The perpetual spray of salt water, along with the heat of summer, the chill of winter, and the strong harbor winds, inevitably took their toll. And not only on the statue itself. By the late 1920s half of the floodlight projectors no longer worked properly, and many had become unmoored and risked being blown out to sea.

A small emergency appropriation of 1931 enabled the War Department to fix the lighting system, replace the creaking elevator, and strengthen the upraised arm. But most of the necessary maintenance remained deferred. Only with the advent of the New Deal and its unprecedented levels of peacetime government spending did the Statue of Liberty gain its first substantial federal appropriation.

FDR's administration made a genuine effort to turn the statue into a landmark hospitable to visitors and a monument of truly national proportions. This government attention to the Statue of Liberty, with its attendant funding for badly needed improvements and repairs, coincided with Lady Liberty's new status as a widely admired symbol of immigration. With massive immigration now relegated to the past, the statue lost its controversial character and could now embody a nation no longer sharply divided between putatively dangerous and alien newcomers on the one hand and "real Americans" on the other. This emerging consensus around the statue as symbol of the nation helped make it politically possible to devote substantial New Deal resources to its maintenance and eventually its beautification.

The first step was the expansion in 1934 of the National Park Service (NPS), now part of the Department of the Interior, to include historic buildings and monuments. This development ended the old tripartite administration of the Statue of Liberty and its pedestal, but it still left the rest of Bedloe's Island under the jurisdiction of the army, which presided over a dilapidated military installation there. Nowadays, Liberty Island, as the old Bedloe's is called, sparkles with green landscaped lawns that gently slope downward from the statue's base to the broad walkway that surrounds it. Liberty has nothing underfoot. Back in the 1930s she stood amid an unsightly cluster of nearly three dozen warehouses, barracks, administrative and utility buildings, and miscellaneous sheds. Passengers disembarking from the Manhattan ferry immediately were confronted by a smelly "comfort station" and a rusting metallic hotdog stand. No wonder only a small number of tourists visited the island.[2]

The NPS wanted to give the Statue of Liberty the dignified surroundings she deserved, but first it had to wrest Bedloe's Island from the army. The process took until the fall of 1937, when Roosevelt proclaimed the entire island part of the Statue of Liberty national monument. Meanwhile, the NPS devised an ambitious plan to remove all structures save for the statue itself, shore up the island with a new seawall and landfill, build a new dock, add walkways around the monument, and finally repair or replace badly rusted parts of Liberty's skeleton. The Park Service didn't possess the $1.5 million needed to do this work, so it relied on New Deal institutions designed to alleviate unemployment and bolster the economy by dispatching people to public works projects. Between 1937 and 1941, the Public Works Administration (PWA) and Works Progress Administration (WPA) sent hundreds of laborers to Bedloe's Island to fulfill the NPS's plans. They removed Liberty's rays one by one to clean out the rusted innards that threatened to collapse them into the sea; began work on the corroded, unsafe cast-iron stairway to the top of the pedestal; replaced the dangerous steps that led up to the statue's base; sealed Liberty's footings with a copper apron designed to keep seawater and rainwater out; remodeled the administration building; and built a visitors' center.

Work proceeded relatively quickly until December 1941, when the Japanese attacked Pearl Harbor. For the next four years, the federal government focused its energies and resources on the war, leaving most repair, conservation, and beautification projects, including the Statue of Liberty, unfinished. But the war abroad, and soon the war effort at home, promoted the statue to the symbolic center of the United States. Throughout the 1930s the U.S. government, pressured by public opinion and its own officials' hostility to foreigners, had been extremely reluctant to admit menaced Jews and other refugees. But by 1940 the war in Europe and the widespread oppression and suffering of people subjected to German occupation had changed American attitudes. Citizens now showed more willingness to welcome foreigners (although very few could find ways to escape Europe), and editorialists nationwide expressed sympathy for the Europeans' plight as well as pride in their country as a refuge for those who hoped to elude Hitler's net. As for the recent immigrants themselves, even those who had suffered from prejudice and discrimination in the United States now felt a renewed gratitude toward their adopted country.

These developments added all the more to the Statue of Liberty's luster as symbol not only of American welcome and openness but of an essential American identity itself. Visits to the statue jumped 42 percent between the last year of peace and the first of the war, and Bedloe's Island set an all-time record for a single twenty-four-hour period, with 9,211 visits on Labor Day 1940. The overall numbers rose still higher in 1941, making the Statue of Liberty, as the *New York Times* put it, "our No. 1 Symbol."[3]

The statue's prestige spilled over into the postwar years, when annual visits hit five hundred thousand and continued to climb. Liberty tourism would breach the one million mark in 1964.[4] It stands at three to four million annually today. The huge number of visitors called attention to the unfinished state of Bedloe's Island and to the ailing statue itself. In 1946, Pulitzer's successor paper, the *World-Telegram*, excoriated the NPS for "the unkempt condition of this revered monument," for a neglect that "borders on a national disgrace."[5] Exaggerated as they were, these angry words moved Congress to appropriate enough to finish the projects begun before the war. The NPS demolished all remaining extraneous buildings, dredged a channel for larger ferryboats, and landscaped the island. Although workmen addressed some of the statue's structural problems, the postwar appropriation, relatively healthy as it was, could provide only temporary solutions. The reality was that Eiffel's original iron skeleton, innovative for its time, didn't meet mid-twentieth-century standards. It had rusted badly and would need to be replaced. That enormous, complex project would have to await a centennial celebration still more than thirty years away.

In the meantime, Liberty's popularity—and the reverence surrounding it—continued to grow. By the mid-1950s, the Statue of Liberty began to figure prominently on U.S. postage stamps. And the country's history of immigration now basked in a glow of nostalgia made possible by what seemed the definitive end of the influx from abroad. Since 1924, Ellis Island had received only a trickle of newcomers; it closed altogether in 1954. With immigration now apparently relegated to the past, Americans could celebrate it symbolically by making the Statue of Liberty into *the* icon of America. But for many commentators, such a symbolic commemoration didn't do justice to what now seemed fundamental to the American identity itself. We needed to reexperience our immigrant heritage, and to do that, a number of influential people now argued, only a museum of American immigration would do. Where to put that museum seemed obvious: it would go inside the Statue of Liberty. Putting it there would strengthen the monument's symbolic tie to immigration all the more, while adding the concrete connections to the immigrant experience that genuine historical artifacts were said to supply. As representatives of the NPS wrote at the time, "The foot of our great symbol of the American ideal was the most appropriate place for presenting the fruits of that ideal."[6]

To build the museum, in 1954 a group of blue-ribbon New Yorkers created the National Committee for the American Museum of Immigration (AMI). Its first presidents were the industrialist Pierre S. Du Pont III and Major General Ulysses S. Grant III, grandson of the president whom Bartholdi had met on his maiden voyage to the United States. Two years later, Congress endorsed the proposed immigration museum and voted to rename the dot of land that anchors Bartholdi's monument Liberty Island. A joint House-Senate resolution proclaimed: "The Statue of Liberty is to the world the symbol of the dreams and aspirations which have drawn so many millions of immigrants to America."[7]

These noble words, like the sentiments expressed when an earlier Congress first accepted Bartholdi's gift, came without any significant funding attached. As the pedestal committee had done three-quarters of a century earlier, the AMI resolved to raise funds for the museum project privately. Prominent journalists supported the idea, and the famed television host Edward R. Murrow devoted a show to the project. But the fund-raising effort went nowhere: in more than a decade it netted less than $.5 million. The National Park Service ultimately contributed some money but devoted it mainly to enlarging the pedestal's foundation and improving access to the statue for the growing number of visitors. The NPS also created a small exhibition space and eventually coaxed a series of federal appropriations totaling $5 million, enough to build a modest museum.[8]

For once with the Statue of Liberty, the main problem didn't revolve around funding. Instead, the American Museum of Immigration became ensnared in ideology, in the dramatic changes in the public discourse surrounding immigration that surfaced in the 1960s. In the mid-1950s, when elite New Yorkers first conceived the museum, most journalists and historians understood immigration to the United States as having created a "melting pot," a mixture of different peoples who melded together to form a unified American identity. As the AMI's Historians Committee and NPS directors put it in 1954, the museum should focus on "Americanization," on the "flowing together of the various races, creeds and cultures into one main stream."[9] Such, at least, was how most prominent commentators of the 1950s described immigration's results. In practice, Americans commonly divided themselves according to their country of origin and often avoided, or discriminated against, those deemed to have come from inferior places. Thus, Americans of Irish background often felt ill-treated by people originally from England. Germans not infrequently looked down on Poles; Jews found themselves excluded from top universities and country clubs (while German Jews looked down on their eastern European coreligionists); and African Americans faced harsh Jim Crow laws in the South and racism in the North and West.

Despite such divisions, in the Cold War atmosphere of the mid-1950s the historian chosen to prepare the AMI's prospectus, Thomas M. Pitkin, envisaged a museum designed to build national unity in the face of military and ideological threats from abroad. "In a time of conflicting ideologies," Pitkin wrote, "when the competition for the loyalties of groups and individuals is keen," the AMI would emphasize the immigrants' contributions to a "common national life." By immigrants, Pitkin mostly meant those who had come from Europe during the nineteenth and early twentieth centuries. He implicitly excluded from the story he planned to tell the millions of involuntary immigrants from Africa, the Chinese and Japanese who had mostly settled on the West Coast, and the growing number of Puerto Ricans and other Spanish-speakers who had begun to flow into the United States. Throughout most of its history, the U.S. census didn't even count the number of foreign-born people whose native language was Spanish. When it began to do so consistently in 1970, Spanish-speakers had already reached 19 percent of the 9.6 million foreign-born individuals residing in this country.[10] The proportion of Spanish-speakers would hit almost 40 percent in 1990.

But in 1958, when Pitkin and other museum planners first presented what we would now call their "Eurocentric" conception of the exhibits, most commentators accepted their premises at face value. A half-dozen years later, such an approach already seemed hopelessly out of date. The civil rights movement had focused attention on Americans of African origin and made it impossible to sustain the triumphalist narrative of immigrant assimilation and success that underlay the story Pitkin intended to tell. The new assertiveness and cultural pride of black Americans encouraged members of other minority groups to delve into their own ethnic histories, detail the hardships and discrimination their forebears had faced, and celebrate their distinctiveness rather than what they shared with other citizens of the United States.

These developments both sparked and expressed a democratization of American universities, which had begun to admit students from the lower reaches of the middle class. Many of the new students belonged to ethnic minorities, some of whom began to explore their cultural roots. Those who became historians commonly turned to a "new social history" attuned to race and ethnicity (and eventually to women and gender).[11] This "history from the bottom up" rejected the metaphor of America as a melting pot. Immigration now seemed rather to have produced what the historian Robert Ernst called a "salad bowl," a mixture of distinctive ingredients tossed together without losing the colors, qualities, textures, shapes, and sizes that made them unique.[12] In this view, immigration had not produced a harmonious blend of different peoples, but a mosaic of cultural diversity and ethnic pluralism.

The AMI planners, having conceived their museum just before these developments erupted onto the American scene, remained wedded to their original ideas. They remained so partly for bureaucratic reasons—once enmeshed in the NPS machinery, museum organizers found it difficult to change gears—and partly for ideological ones. The museum planners inhabited a mental universe influenced neither by academic history nor by the representatives of newly mobilized ethnic groups. When museum officials finally tried to take the new claims into account, their efforts proved clumsy at best. An initial AMI exhibit of 1965 referred to black Americans as involuntary immigrants and pictured them as abject beings crammed beneath the deck of a miserable slave ship. This portrait evoked an angry response from New York Congressman Adam Clayton Powell, who denounced the exhibit as an "insult . . . to America's 20,000,000 Negroes." It portrayed blacks only as brutalized and oppressed, ignoring the "fantastic cultural contributions of Negroes in this country."[13]

These remarks foreshadowed a great many more to come. In 1967 Eugene Kusielewicz, vice president of the Kosciuszko Foundation, complained bitterly that "a visitor would leave the proposed museum with the impression that the two largest immigrant groups [Poles and Italians] virtually do not exist." Italian American notables leveled similar charges and echoed Powell in protesting the banal, stereotyped imagery of their ethnic group. Congressman Frank Annunzio charged that when AMI planners didn't ignore Italians altogether, they pictured them only as fisherman and vineyard workers "enjoying an Italian dinner." Annunzio wanted the AMI to delete "the entire text about spaghetti, eggplant, peppers, Chianti, pizza, etc."[14]

Meanwhile, Jewish leaders protested the exclusive reliance on religious artifacts in the proposed exhibit, while others objected to the near-neglect of Mexican, French Canadian, and Asian immigrants. Another criticism came from historians and journalists who represented the new social history. Rudolph J. Vecoli, who directed the new Center for Immigration Studies at the University of Minnesota, denounced "the Museum's emphasis on the elite, [on] the few who won fame and fortune." He wanted the exhibit to pay attention to the "millions of ordinary people" who had made immigration to the United States a "folk movement of unprecedented dimensions."[15]

When NPS curator David Wallace lamely responded in mid-1971 that it was too late to refocus the exhibit, Vecoli mobilized the leaders of Polish, Italian, Jewish, and other organizations to help him create "a nationwide campaign against the Museum concept." The campaign never materialized, but Vecoli convened a group of distinguished historians and representatives of the various ethnic groups, who prepared a highly critical evaluation of the AMI's plans. NPS leaders responded with a few, mostly cosmetic changes but remained yoked to a set of premises about U.S. immigration now almost twenty years out of date.

If the new AMI disappointed a great many scholars, President Richard Nixon seemed more than pleased. He decided to speak at the museum's dedication on September 26, 1972, seeking, as the New York *Daily News* put it, "the ethnic vote which usually goes to the Democrats" in the upcoming presidential election. The president's advisers turned the dedication into an "ethnic festival" complete with young girls dressed in the "traditional" costumes of Italy, Germany, Poland, and Ukraine. Press reaction to the dedication and to the museum itself was predictably mixed. New York editorialists generally liked it, but the Philadelphia *Evening Bulletin*, among other papers, found it wanting. "What was the big rush to open this travesty?" asked the *Bulletin*'s reporter, Rose De Wolf. "The overall impression you get there is that there are two ways to prove yourself as an American—one is to become rich and famous and the other— not as good—is to die in a war. Women and children, needless to say, are rarely in view. Poor Miss Liberty. What a dirty trick to hide this under her skirt."[16]

Tourists' views seemed mixed as well. Less than half of those who visited the statue bothered to enter the museum, and those who did spent an average of just 17.9 minutes there. To see everything would have taken 60 to 90 minutes.[17] Still, an informal survey indicated than many liked what they saw and showed particular interest in the exhibits devoted to their own ethnic groups. Although permanently strapped for funds, the AMI curators made some effort to represent ordinary people and not just elites by collecting and displaying amateur photographs and films, and especially by recording the oral histories of more than 150 people who had entered the United States through Ellis Island.

If the American Museum of Immigration proved only a modest success, it helped set the stage for a vastly more important—and successful—project: the restoration of the main immigration reception center on Ellis Island and creation of a magnificent museum there, a project that took almost three decades to complete.[18] Had the federal government's original intentions been fulfilled, it would never have been done at all. After the Immigration and Naturalization Service closed Ellis Island in November 1954, the government decided to sell the island to the highest bidder. The General Services Administration (GSA) advertised the property in the *Wall Street Journal*, calling it "one of the most famous landmarks in the world." Its potential uses? "Oil storage depot, import and export processing, warehousing, manufacturing"—twenty-seven acres of land, thirty-five buildings, and even the ferryboat "Ellis Island" formed part of the deal. The GSA advertised the sale widely, so widely that it evoked a storm of protest. "To millions and millions of Americans," wrote one angry former immigrant, "Ellis Island was the 19th and 20th century counterpart of Plymouth Rock. . . . To see it sold for commercial purposes will be to see it lose its identity and its historic memory." Politicians quickly weighed in, among them the New York congressman T. James Tumulty, who said, "If you can auction off Ellis Island, perhaps you will be auctioning off the Statue of Liberty next."[19]

President Dwight Eisenhower quickly suspended the sale, a move that seemed to please almost everyone except those promoting the American Museum of Immigration. "It is inconceivable," declared AMI co-chairs David McDonald and Du Pont, that Ellis Island "should be considered as appropriate for a national tribute to immigration." This statement sounds bizarre today, but in the mid-1950s Ellis Island, which had housed illegal immigrants awaiting deportation before World War II and foreigners deemed subversive afterward, appeared to the AMI promoters a "depository of bad memories."[20] Du Pont and his colleagues also feared that a restoration of the old immigration center would compete with their plans to establish a museum on Liberty Island. But with the AMI progressing slowly, Du Pont's views convinced neither Congress nor the administrations of Presidents John F. Kennedy and Lyndon Johnson. In 1965 Johnson announced that Ellis Island would become part of the Statue of Liberty National Monument and that Jobs Corps workers would be dispatched to Ellis to help fix it up.

But government funds quickly dried up in the face of mounting expenditures on the war in Vietnam, and it would take tens of millions of dollars in private contributions for Ellis Island to become the impressive museum of immigration we know today. The highly successful Ellis Island restoration lies beyond the scope of this book, but it is important to note that the museum there presents an ideal complement to the Statue of Liberty, which has transferred much of its immigration symbolism to the island next door. One result is that the statue can now stand apart from our renewed controversies over immigration and represent the more abstract ideals Bartholdi originally had in mind.

EIGHT

The Popular Imagination

If the federal government has often neglected the Statue of Liberty, such was not true of the public at large, especially in the twentieth century. Tourism there didn't begin to soar until after 1945, but even before Bartholdi erected his statue in New York Harbor, journalists, cartoonists, playwrights, photographers, painters, advertisers, and many others couldn't get enough of it. Tens of thousands, as we've seen, flocked to the U.S. centennial celebration in Philadelphia to see Liberty's arm and torch. They bought reams of sheet music with the monument on the cover; countless illustrated magazines and newspapers; and Liberty trinkets, postcards, and other souvenirs by the boatload. Later, nearly a dozen postage stamps would feature Lady Liberty, and she would become an irresistible prop or symbol for filmmakers great and obscure. Advertisers grabbed hold of the great green goddess from the beginning and never let go.

Bartholdi's Statue of Liberty coincided almost exactly with the advent of the advertising agent, the nineteenth-century predecessor of the "Mad Men" of Madison Avenue. These agents took advantage of the ubiquity of Liberty's image, even before the statue itself went up. One obvious early use was to sell French products in the

"Elite 'Sec' Champagne Enlightening the World" (*Judge*, October 30, 1886).

United States—champagne, for example, and other Parisian luxury goods as well. At first, advertisers took existing images of the statue and added a caption touting their product, as they did for "Astral Oil," using the Root and Tinker print originally commissioned by the U.S. fund-raising committee. In other cases, advertisers altered a ready-made image to feature what they wanted to sell. Most often, they replaced Liberty's torch with their product so the statue could appear to hold it aloft. Using an 1883 Currier and Ives lithograph, "Star Lamps" turned the torch into one of its lights. Some switches

LET THE ADVERTISING AGENTS TAKE CHARGE OF THE BARTHOLDI BUSINESS,
AND THE MONEY WILL BE RAISED WITHOUT DELAY.

Liberty as advertising billboard: "Let the advertising agents take charge of the Bartholdi business, and the money will be raised without delay" (*Puck*).

seemed less germane—as when Liberty held aloft St. Jacob's Oil and Perry's laundry soap. And in other cases, the entire statue morphed into the product in question, as in Dr. Hass Hog Remedy (1884), which transformed Liberty into a pig. Such near vulgarity moved *Puck* magazine to mock the situation by plastering ads over every inch of Liberty's form.

Unsurprisingly, the idea of liberty appears as a key theme in advertisements using Bartholdi's sculpture. In 1883, Singer sewing machines put out a three-by-five-inch "trade card" showing the statue on one side and the following text on the other:

> If the WOMEN of the world were to build a monument to com-
> memorate that which had afforded them the greatest liberty,
> and given them the most time for enlightening their minds and
> those of their children, they would build one to the SEWING
> MACHINE, which has released the Mother of the Race from
> countless hours of weary drudgery, and has in the truest and
> best sense been quietly but steadily *Enlightening the World.*[1]

If Singer liberated women from drudgery, L & M cigarettes, according to a late-1950s ad, freed them from the ill effects of tar and
from the aging process as well. The Statue of Liberty is "still young
and beautiful at age 75," just as you can be by smoking the cigarette
that's "light, mild . . . and *kindest to your taste.*"

It's easy to smile at ads such as these, at Statues of Liberty slurp-
ing an ice cream cone instead of holding a torch, or at a barcode that
takes Liberty's form. Artists and cartoonists have long made a sport
of satirizing the statue's naked commercial use. Robert O. Blechman's send-up of McDonald's turns the statue's crown into the
company's iconic golden arches, and he captions the cartoon, "Over
17 billion served." This droll image pairs nicely with a real French
advertisement for that country's own fast-food chain "Quick." The
text beside Liberty's face explains how Bartholdi's sculpture
"amazed" the Americans, just as the quality of Quick burgers must
amaze us as well. Taking all this in, the French painter Jean Lagarrigue produced a particularly unsubtle commentary on the commercialization of the Statue of Liberty as symbol of a commercialistic
United States. His Liberty reshapes itself into a Coke bottle holding a torch. The tablet has been erased, suggesting that July 4, 1776,
has lost all meaning save for the freedom to buy and sell. Better
perhaps than this brutal satire is an advertising image lacking in any

Robert O. Blechman, *Over 17 Billion Served* (1974). (Courtesy of the artist)

(overt) satirical intent: an all-purpose inflatable Liberty that allows the icon to stand for any product or service an advertiser wants.

For all its commercial exploitation, Bartholdi's sculpture has also been used to publicize more serious things, especially during times of war. The most famous such ads are for the Liberty Loans that helped finance the First World War. One asks potential contributors to "Remember Your First Thrill of American Liberty," and another

Jean Lagarrigue, *Miss Liberty/Coca Cola*. (Courtesy of the artist)

urges "that liberty shall not perish from the earth." Later, America First-ers used Liberty's image to disseminate their isolationist message, while in 1942 she encouraged young men to prepare for combat by joining the Boy Scouts. Two years later, she stood for the liberation of France.

The Statue of Liberty's versatility, her status as a "hollow icon" open to almost any meaning, allowed her to stand just as easily for peace as for war, for the virtues of unrestricted immigration and the dangers of admitting huddled masses from abroad. Liberty bonds encouraged the war effort in 1917, but in the composer Kurt Weill's hands two decades later, the statue bore witness to the evils of battle. Weill's first U.S. musical, *Johnny Johnson* (1936, lyrics by Paul Green), portrays Liberty as the opposite of a warm, open-armed

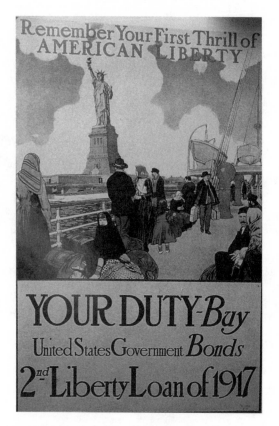

Liberty loan poster, 1917.

"Mother of Exiles." She's the stone-cold symbol of needless death, "a meaningless, insensate" form used to justify sending young men to war.

In the final scene of act I, Johnny finds himself en route to the trenches of France, thinking, among other things, about his fiancée, Minny Belle.[2] As his ship begins its journey to the Old World in early 1918, it passes the Statue of Liberty. "The upper part of her figure," reads the stage directions, appears "illuminated from a hid-

R. Dumoulin, *Liberation*, 1944. (FR 1721 [OS], Poster collection,
Hoover Institution Archives)

den light. . . . Tall and majestic she stands, immovable, and brood-
ing over the scene like some fabled apocalyptic figure."

Dressed in an army uniform, Johnny, "his rumpled hair gently
caressed by a little breeze . . . [stares] in dreamy and silent awe at the
faraway STATUE." After a moment, he begins to speak:

There you stand,
Like a picture in that history book I read.

Minny Belle said I'd see you so,
And now at last I have—
Your hand uplifted with a torch
Saying goodbye to us,
Good luck and bless you everyone.
(*with hushed fervency*)
And God bless you,
O Mother of Liberty—
That's what you are,
A sort of mother to us all,
(*saluting sharply*)
And we your sons.
And here tonight as we set forth
To fight the German Lords.

His speech complete, Johnny stretches out among the other sleeping figures on the deck. The stage directions point to the illuminated statue, "alone in the depths of the night, lonely and aloof." Suddenly she comes to life: "a shiver seems to run through her figure, and quietly she begins to turn as if following with her sightless, stony stare the progress of the boat that carries JOHNNY JOHNSON out to sea. And as if up from the caverns of her hollow breast, a vast and all-pervasive whispering sigh goes out over the scene." Having heard Johnny's lines, Liberty begins to sing, "her voice tinged with a queer, outlandish quality of sound through stone:"

He calls on me, poor wandering one,
A voice more piteous than the rest,
And knows not I'm a thing of stone
And have no heart within my breast.

A million years I dreamless lay
Insensate in the quiet earth,

Unformed and will-less till the day
Men rived me forth and gave me birth.

And set me up with queer intent
To swear their pride and folly by,
And I who never nothing meant
Am used to send men forth to die.

Clearly, the lyricist didn't know much about the Statue of Liberty, thinking her made of stone, but for him, the stony earth symbolized the body-strewn trenches in which so many young lives had come to an end. The mediocre writing and sodden music makes it unsurprising that Weill's first U.S. composition left little lasting impression here. But in the late 1930s it enjoyed a certain popularity, if not critical acclaim, logging sixty-six performances on Broadway and dozens more in Boston, Los Angeles, and elsewhere after it became part of the New Deal's Federal Theatre Project in 1937.

If the Weill/Green musical represented the Statue of Liberty's Broadway debut, she earned a second starring role in 1949 amid the patriotic afterglow of the Second World War. The great songwriter Irving Berlin teamed up with the playwright Robert E. Sherwood, director Moss Hart, and choreographer Jerome Robbins to produce a showy musical titled *Miss Liberty*. The plot was banal—two newspapers competing to discover who had been Bartholdi's model for Liberty's face. But the play proved popular thanks in part to a grand finale in which the entire cast sang "Give Me Your Tired, Your Poor" beneath a shimmering shadow of the goddess of New York.[3]

By 1949 the statue had been fully Americanized, its French origins largely forgotten on this side of the Atlantic. The "Liberty Loan" posters of World War I had begun the process of Americanization, as—somewhat ironically—had the end of mass immigration in 1924. By the 1940s, the children and grandchildren of the turn-of-the-century wave of newcomers had themselves been Americanized,

Cover of *Life*, June 5, 1939. (Herbert Gehr/Getty Images)

and that helped the immigrants' monumental symbol be Americanized as well. As for World War II, it cemented the identification of
the Statue of Liberty with the United States. When Nazi Germany
subdued most of Europe and threatened Great Britain, it seemed to
many Americans that their country might soon become the world's
last bastion of liberty. *Life* expressed this view with a cover image of
the Statue of Liberty photographed to show it looming over New
York Harbor as a "fortress of freedom," as the mighty guardian of a
great continental power immune from Hitler's designs. "It is fitting,"

wrote *Life*'s editors, "that in these days when the light of freedom burns ever lower in Europe, Liberty stands out with new brightness against the American sky."[4]

Two years into World War II, *Life*'s image of fortress Liberty jumped from its front cover to one of Alfred Hitchcock's best wartime films, *Saboteur* (1942).[5] The British-born director began work on the movie almost immediately after the attack on Pearl Harbor, and he concluded it with a dramatic chase scene in—and on—the Statue of Liberty, used as a prop for making an uplifting political point. The plot revolves around a clean-cut American worker, Barry Kane (Robert Cummings), falsely accused of being a German agent and sabotaging an aircraft factory near Los Angeles. Kane thinks he knows who really committed the crime, and he escapes police custody to pursue the real German agent, a man named Fry (Norman Lloyd). During the chase, Kane meets a beautiful model, Pat Martin (Priscilla Lane), who alternately believes and disbelieves Kane's story. Once in New York, Kane foils Fry's attempt to blow up an American warship, and for inexplicable reasons the saboteur then boards a ferry for the Statue of Liberty. Martin follows him onto the boat. The camera shows us the monument looming in the water, but Fry turns his back to it. The German agent has no interest in what Liberty represents.

Martin tails Fry into the statue, and both climb to the top. The FBI has told her to stall him until the G-men can get there. Trying to make conversation, she tells him it's the first time she's been to the statue: "It means so much to us now." The French gave it to us, she adds, "but just look at the French [now]; isn't it sad?"—a reference to the German occupation of France and the collaborationist Vichy regime. She then recites the first stanza of Emma Lazarus's poem. But Fry can only scoff: "Oh, little Miss Liberty carrying the torch." Martin tries to charm him into remaining with her, but he finds out who she is and flees, first down the winding stairs and then

Good-guy Barry Kane (Robert Cummings) hangs on to the torch with one hand as he attempts to rescue the villain (Norman Lloyd) with the other in Alfred Hitchcock's 1942 thriller, *Saboteur.* (Everett Collection, Inc.)

up into the torch. Kane, now on the scene, follows him there, armed with a gun that Fry had dropped earlier. We see the two men on the narrow platform surrounding the flame. The German agent backs away from Kane and topples over the low railing. He manages to grab hold of Liberty's arm, and Kane risks his life to save him. A wide camera shot shows the two men clinging tenuously to the arm; an overhead view reveals just how high up they are. Kane holds Fry by his sleeve, and a close-up shows the seam coming apart. Seconds later, the German agent plummets to his death, as if vanquished by the Statue of Liberty and all she represents.

Hitchcock's political purposes are clear, and his use of the Statue of Liberty as the scene of danger and suspense foreshadows the appearance of another great American monument, Mount Rushmore, in the concluding sequences of *North by Northwest* (1959).[6] Here, Cary Grant and Eva Marie Saint flee two villains by descending precariously across Lincoln's nose. Both villains plummet from the monument, while the heroes come through the ordeal, as in *Saboteur*, alive and in love. It's notable that, in 1942, Hitchcock didn't imagine that Liberty herself might be the target of a saboteur. In his day, terrorists attacked factories and soldiers and sometimes civilians, but not symbols. In our time, the Statue of Liberty's thick blanket of security, far stricter than at airports, ballparks, and other vulnerable places, suggests that today's terrorism has heavily symbolic designs, though it of course takes a terrible toll on human lives as well.

Hitchcock proved to be the first of many filmmakers to bring the image, idea, and symbolism of the Statue of Liberty into their work. After *Saboteur*, the most famous use of the statue is doubtless the shot that concludes *Planet of the Apes* (1968). Charlton Heston escapes from the Ape civilization and makes his way to a forbidden part of the planet. There he rides horseback along a sparkling water's edge, accompanied by a mute, animal-brained human female—in this topsy-turvy world, the human-ape hierarchy has been reversed. Suddenly we see a twisted piece of metal from behind and then four dark spokes pointing toward the sky. The camera zooms in and frames Heston between the two middle spokes. "Oh my God," he cries, "I'm back, I'm home. . . . You finally, really did it . . . you blew it up. . . . Goddamn you all to Hell!" The camera pans up and away from Heston, and we see the ruined upper half of the Statue of Lib-

The final scene in *Planet of the Apes* (1968). (Everett Collection, Inc.)

erty emerging from the sandy shore. Her broken image reveals to the hero that he'd been on Earth all along—a post-apocalyptic Earth, a wrecked human civilization, apparently destroyed in a holocaust exemplified by Liberty's severed torso. The remains of Miss Liberty make a stark contrast with Heston's mute, uncomprehending companion, for Liberty alone is full of human meaning. The silent statue, not the voiceless female, serves as exemplar of a great civilization that has destroyed itself.[7]

Another mute, clueless woman appears before a looming Statue of Liberty in the movie *Splash* (1984). Daryl Hannah plays a mermaid who emerges from New York Harbor and slips onto Liberty Island, naked and suddenly transformed into completely human form. Naturally, the gorgeous unclad blonde diverts the tourists' attention away from the monument and onto her. Is this an indication, this time playful, of the perils civilization faces? How can Lady Liberty, who represents austere ideals and solemn promises, compete with pure Eros, however innocent? In both *Planet of the Apes* and *Splash*, the real woman represents untamed, unintelligent nature—as women have often been made to do in Western culture—while the allegorical, lifeless statue stands in for human civilization.

The 2011 film *The Adjustment Bureau* reiterates such themes by having the hero, a charismatic young politician named David Norris (Matt Damon), lead an uncomprehending "natural" woman, Elise Sellas (Emily Blunt), a sensuous dancer, onto Liberty Island. The Adjustment Bureau represents Fate, or God's design, and fate has decreed that for Norris to win the presidency (which the Adjustment Bureau wants), David and Elise must be kept apart. Agents of the bureau are prepared to take extreme measures to confine David to his preordained path. But the couple falls deeply in love, and a rogue employee of the Adjustment Bureau helps David defy the Plan. That defiance takes place on Liberty Island, where David and Elise open a door into the Statue of Liberty. Once inside, the couple passes into a realm of forbidden free will where they must outwit men with supernatural powers bent on stopping them. Here, the statue represents the terrifying dangers—and ultimate rewards—of resisting authority, foiling fate, and freely choosing one's own path in life. David was destined to be president, though only by sacrificing love. In good Hollywood style, he succeeds in achieving both.

While *Splash* and *The Adjustment Bureau* associate the Statue of Liberty with the perils of love, *Planet of the Apes* was the first of a series of films in which the Statue of Liberty would bear witness to apocalypse and the destruction of New York. A key example is John Carpenter's *Escape from New York* (1981), whose dystopian action is set in 1997 during the concluding phases of World War III. Much of the country has apparently been destroyed, and crime is so severe that authorities have turned a bombed-out Manhattan Island into a huge, walled-in prison camp. Carpenter was the first fiction filmmaker permitted to shoot on Liberty Island, which serves in the film as the remote command post for Manhattan's security forces—no policeman dared to set foot in the city/prison itself. Here Carpenter reverses the Statue of Liberty's dominant symbolism, turning her into the guard tower from which soldiers ensure that no one escapes from New York.

Although Carpenter's film doesn't depict the statue being destroyed, her severed head appeared on the studio's publicity poster. That image apparently inspired J. J. Abrams's film *Cloverfield* (2008), which makes New York the scene of an attack from outer space. An alien ship targets the Statue of Liberty, whose severed head explodes missilelike into the city, where it careens down the streets. *Cloverfield*'s poster shows the statue from behind and shorn of her head. Here Liberty symbolizes the destruction of New York. It's a potent, terrifying image, one that may have influenced New York and federal officials after 9/11. After all, enemies of the United States had, at one point, come close to knocking the Statue of Liberty off its pedestal. On July 30, 1916, with the German army stalemated in France, the Kaiser's agents blew up a munitions dump in Jersey City in an effort to disrupt the supply of shells to Britain and France. The blast sent shock waves as far as Philadelphia and registered the equivalent of a 5.0 earthquake on the Richter scale. The Statue of Liberty was close enough to suffer $2 million in damage, including the weakening of the torch, already unstable from the flawed construction process. Officials made the torch off-limits to visitors, as it has remained ever since. (For that reason, Hitchcock's villain, in real life, wouldn't have been able to climb to the torch and then plunge to his death from there.)

Although the statue suffered indirect damage from the bombing of 1916, it might have been blown up altogether in 1964 when a small group of African American militants teamed up with Quebec separatists to plot the destruction of three icons of America: the Statue of Liberty, the Liberty Bell, and the Washington Monument. The conspirators seemed most intent on blowing away the head and torch of what they termed the "damned old bitch" in New York Harbor. Fortunately, they were clumsy and allowed the group to be infiltrated by undercover agents, who foiled their plans. But their efforts, futile as they were, seemed to encourage others to use the Statue of Liberty for militant, if less-destructive, ends.

On the day after Christmas 1971, fifteen members of the group Vietnam Veterans Against the War hid inside the pedestal just before closing time. Once the tourists had gone, the veterans seized control of the monument and promised to remain there until President Nixon ended the war. After a lengthy standoff with the police, the protestors agreed to leave peacefully. "The reason we chose the Statue of Liberty," declared the group's final communiqué, "is that since we were children, the statue has been analogous in our minds with freedom and an America we love. Then we went to fight a war in the name of freedom. We saw that freedom is . . . allowed only to those who are white and maintain the status quo."[8] The Vietnam veterans staged their sit-in at the Statue of Liberty not because they found the monument hypocritical, as had the earlier group, but because it dramatized to them how much the country had fallen short of its ideals.

Three years after the Vietnam veterans' occupation, another radical group, the Attica Brigade, locked itself inside the statue, calling for Nixon's resignation. (He ultimately left office, of course, but not because of them.) In 1976, antiwar veterans took over the monument once again, and a few months later dissident Iranians seized the statue in protest of U.S. support for the shah. Law enforcement agents got both groups to leave peacefully, only to have a dozen Puerto Rican nationalists take their place. For the most part, the various groups of protestors used the statue to dramatize their respective causes; they did no damage to the monument itself. But bomb threats against the statue were common in the 1970s, and in June 1980 a band of Croatian terrorists succeeded in setting off an explosive device. They destroyed parts of Liberty's base, but fortunately no one was inside. Only in the 1980s did the Park Service tighten security enough to prevent recurring occupations and attacks. Local and federal officials had come to understand that the Statue of Liberty represented a choice political target, but not until September 11, 2001, did they perceive that terrorists might want to destroy it altogether.

Immediately following Al Qaeda's assault on the Twin Towers and the Pentagon, the National Park Service closed Liberty Island, fearing a potential attempt against the statue. The island remained off-limits for three months, and the statue itself was closed until August 2004. Visitors weren't allowed to climb to Liberty's crown until July 2009. By then the Park Service had introduced strict new security protocols that, among other things, restricted to about two hundred a day the number of people allowed to climb above the pedestal. September 11 may have awakened government officials to the mortal dangers facing the Statue of Liberty, but filmmakers had begun to create fantasy versions of such threats long before that fateful date.

Already in 1987, *GI Joe: The Movie* depicted the prospect of a terrorist attack on the goddess of the harbor. The evil Cobra organization plans to blow the statue up, and only at the last minute does the film's hero manage to foil the plot. In another 1987 movie, *Superman IV*, the man of steel almost dies while protecting Lady Liberty from Nuclear Man's wrath, and in *Batman Forever* (1995) villains crash a helicopter into her.

Although these dangers come from Earth, Liberty's cinematic enemies have mostly hailed from other worlds. In *Independence Day* (1996), a gargantuan flying saucer vaporizes New York and knocks the Statue of Liberty on her side. *Deep Impact* (1998) shoots a comet into midtown Manhattan, its shock wave producing a tsunami that propels Liberty's severed head (again) through the gutted city. Steven Spielberg's *Artificial Intelligence* (2001) buries Bartholdi's monument under water up to her torch. But that's nothing compared to the indignities she suffers in Roland Emmerich's *The Day After Tomorrow* (2004), a global warming film that makes Al Gore's *An Inconvenient Truth* seem equivocal by comparison. Emmerich's drama subjects New York to tidal waves and biblical floods before freezing it down to absolute zero. The Statue of Liberty turns into an ice sculpture, her green form now brilliantly white.

While the Statue of Liberty often comes to life in political cartoons, and talks and sings in O. Henry and Kurt Weill stories, she rarely moves about in film. The exception comes in *Ghostbusters II* (1989), when the heroes desperately battle an invasion of supernatural slime. As the ooze draws force, it roars up from the sewers and subway tunnels of New York, taking shape as a pair of monsters determined to destroy the city. Fortunately, the slime isn't inherently bad; when infused with a positive charge, it can combat its dark, evil side. Knowing as much, poltergeist exterminator Bill Murray and company ascend to the Statue of Liberty's crown and blast the monument with positive ooze. Immediately, we see Eiffel's inner structure melt into motion, propelling the statue off its pedestal and across the harbor, the water up to her neck. She then trudges through the city streets, King Kong–like, in pursuit of the monsters, which she helps defeat. In the end, barbarism succumbs, as Liberty, having saved civilization, returns to her perch.[9]

If the statue has regularly faced destruction and dismemberment on film, in countless video games players get the chance to save her from such a fate. She's threatened by German Zeppelins ("Turning Point: Fall of Liberty"), Soviet planes ("Command & Conquer: Red Alert 2," "Freedom Fighters"), nuclear bombs ("Splinter Cell:

Double Agent"), and Japanese terrorists ("Metal Gear Solid 2"). Still, Lady Liberty doesn't necessarily come out unscathed. In "Twisted Metal 2: World Tour," players shoot at the statue until her robes disappear, revealing a red bikini underneath. More gunfire makes her enormously fat while stretching her bikini to the breaking point. In the end, gamers can destroy her completely. Ditto in "Command & Conquer: Red Alert 3," whose object is to demolish the Statue of Liberty and then to build a Lenin statue in her place.

On television, the Statue of Liberty has made a great many cameo appearances, as in *CSI NY,* when blood on her crown revealed that two National Park Service guards had been murdered inside. Viewers could also glimpse her on *The Simpsons, Family Guy,* and *Seinfeld.* Meanwhile, Miss Piggy, the prima donna star of *The Muppet Show,* regularly posed as Lady Liberty. But when a potential contestant on *American Idol* dressed up as the Statue of Liberty and began to sing "New York, New York," show judge Simon Cowell shooed the young crooner offstage.

Video games and television have accustomed people to seeing the Statue of Liberty unclothed, but never as much as advertisements and political cartoons. Legions of commercial artists and cartoonists have transformed the unerotic Mother of the Harbor into an alluring, sexy babe. During the statue's centennial celebration in 1986, an event widely criticized for its commercialization, the statue appeared as a curvaceous blonde wearing a mini-bra, G-string, and see-through hose. She had become, as the *New Republic* put it, "a high-priced corporate tart," the victim, another commentator wrote, of "statuary rape."[10]

Beyond the centennial, scantily clad Statues of Liberty have served almost every imaginable political and commercial purpose. To poke fun at Donald Trump, a cartoonist drew Lady Liberty as a buxom bimbo, the refurbished symbol of a New York City under the billion-

Carlos Devizia, "Statue of Liberty as Stripper." (Artizans Entertainment Inc.)

aire developer's rule. Another artist pictured the statue in a bikini to represent the chilly winds of recession. And a cartoonist used a naked Liberty to criticize intrusive airport security scans, as did cover artists for the *New Republic*. Sometimes the statue's nudity serves no overt purpose at all, except to give her a female sexuality. Examples include a cartoon in which Liberty sheds her copper skin to reveal a bikini, and Hudson Talbott's *Luncheon on the Grass*, a clever send-up of Edouard Manet's famous painting *Déjeuner sur l'herbe*. Talbott de-

New Republic, December 30, 2010. (Copyright © Sean McCabe)

picts a nude Liberty lounging in Central Park alongside the Empire State Building and the Chrysler Building, the remnants of their picnic littering the ground next to her torch.

Having real women pose as the Statue of Liberty hasn't been uncommon, although usually they're fully clothed. But for the cover of *V Magazine*'s "New York issue" (fall 2010), Lady Gaga stripped down to her bra and panties to masquerade as Lady Liberty. The pop singer's hair is teased into the seven spokes of Liberty's crown, and

Hudson Talbott, *Luncheon on the Grass* (1982). (Courtesy of the artist)

the torch shaped into a burning V. "Just as the Statue of Liberty was France's gift to America," wrote *V* editor Stephen Gan, "Gaga is, to us, New York's greatest gift to pop culture and fashion. [She] is also a beacon of the city's creativity and hope . . . a bona fide genius and we can safely declare her our muse." The Statue of Liberty has suffered a great many indignities, but the comparison to Lady Gaga has to be one of the worst.

Even when feminized Statues of Liberty are covered up, female sexuality is often the point. When former New York governor Eliot Spitzer resigned over a prostitution scandal, a cartoon showed him propositioning the Statue of Liberty. An anti–George W. Bush cover

Mad magazine, June 1975, back cover. (From MAD Magazine No. 175
© E. C. Publications, Inc.)

of the *Village Voice* pictured the former president as a vampire biting
poor Liberty's neck. And an even uglier cartoon on the website Protein Wisdom shows a sobbing Liberty having been violated sexually
by Barack Obama.[11] The caption has the president promising to
come back for more. This disturbing image represents the ultra-
right-wing version of what has been a common cartoonist theme,
the violation of liberty by malign political forces, sometimes on the
right and sometimes on the left. These include, among many other

targets, an intrusive FBI, the Patriot Act, the burka, the pope, and Obama's health care law, the object of Protein Wisdom's sexually charged disdain.

Most such images don't go as far. *Mad* magazine good-naturedly parodied the women's lib movement by having the statue discard her bra, and in other cases, Lady Liberty has lent positive associations to women political figures such as Condoleezza Rice, Hillary Clinton, and Sarah Palin. Cartoonists commonly depict Liberty shedding a feminine tear, and they have shown her bottle-feeding crude oil to a baby Uncle Sam or as an overfed American needing to lose weight. It matters that the Statue of Liberty is a woman, and artists and editors never seem to tire of emphasizing, even exploiting, that fact. Through it all, Bartholdi's monument manages to maintain its dignity, its ability to represent cherished values and ideals. If Lady Gaga can't trivialize Lady Liberty, nothing can.

NINE

Restoration

By the 1960s and 1970s, the public's powerful interest in the Statue of Liberty and its status as a magnet for international tourism made it imperative to attend to the monument's physical deterioration. A century of salt spray, sea air, and high winds had made the structure unstable, even dangerous. Still, the American government, struggling with the stagflation of the 1970s and recession of the early '80s, dragged its feet. Only in 1981, when a group of French architects and engineers outlined the statue's serious structural problems, did the effort to restore the monument begin. Soon the National Park Service got involved, as did a private American architectural firm. Ultimately, a new Franco-American Committee, not unlike Bartholdi's original one, took shape to oversee the restoration project. It quickly became clear that the makeover would be expensive, and the committee set out to raise the required funds.

The French authors of the statue's structural assessment possessed impressive credentials. One was a graduate of both the Ecole polytechnique, France's equivalent of MIT, and the Ecole nationale des beaux-arts, the country's leading art and architectural school. Another was a master metallurgical artisan expert in the delicate techniques of hammered copper work. A pair of leading structural and mechanical engineers rounded out the team. To collaborate with the French *groupement*, the Franco-American Committee enlisted an American architectural firm, Swank Hayden Connell, experienced in historic restoration, and the structural engineers Ammann & Whitney.

Despite good intentions on both sides, cultural differences and language barriers made it difficult for the French and American specialists to work together. As is often the case with Franco-American collaborations, the French found the Americans overly practical, too hurried, insufficiently interested in historical accuracy, and unwilling to trust the intuitive knowledge gained from vast artisanal experience. The Americans, meanwhile, considered their French counterparts too enamored of abstract theories and too divorced from the day-to-day considerations of moving the project along. These differences eventually scuttled the original restoration plan in which the French were to oversee the diagnostic and design work, and the Americans the actual restoration project. When relations between the two groups broke down, the U.S. architects and engineers took control of the project and demoted the French from full partners to consultants.

Another reason for the change of leadership turned on the Franco-American Committee's inability to raise much money. It had to compete with the high-powered Statue of Liberty–Ellis Island Foundation, a private, not-for-profit fund-raising corporation created alongside the public Statue of Liberty–Ellis Island Centennial Commission, established by President Ronald Reagan in 1981 to advise the National Park Service on the restoration of the two historic sites. Reagan had appointed Lee Iacocca, the former head of Chrysler, to run the commission, and Iacocca simultaneously served as the foundation's chair. The former auto executive proved an excellent fund-raiser, and the more successful his efforts became, the more control his group wanted over the restoration processes. Eventually, the French withdrew from the restoration effort, which by mid-1984 had become a largely American affair.

Iacocca claimed he would raise funds for the restoration in the same spirit as Pulitzer had shown in championing the pedestal project a century earlier. The newspaperman considered "the dollar of the hard-working mechanic, the railroad laborer or the shop-girl [a] more noble gift, representing more self-sacrifice, than $10,000 would be from any of our millionaires."[1] Iacocca said much the same thing (allowing for inflation): "We should get the school kids, the Boy Scouts and Girl Scouts involved. Each guy sending in five or ten bucks is better than ten corporations sending in a million-each."[2] More than twenty million people, including a great many school-children, did indeed contribute to the restoration. Many included letters with their checks, and a large number addressed their letters to the statue herself. People recalled their awe or joy in seeing Liberty for the first time, and they wrote about the oppression and hardship, including at Ellis Island, they and their families had suffered before entering the United States. "I first saw you on the evening of May 4, 1909," wrote Olaf Holen, "from the deck of the Immigrant Ship that brought me from Norway. I was wondering . . . 'What is going to happen to me?' . . . But you gave me courage." Another donor remembered, "[You] were a beautiful sight after a miserable crossing that September," and still another recalled, "A boy was screaming with joy, 'Wake up, wake up, you can see the Statue of Liberty. You can see the Statue of Liberty.'"[3]

Immigrants retained vivid memories of their first glimpse of the Statue of Liberty because of the difficult conditions they had escaped. "In 1910," wrote Bluma Clara Fietz, "I came with my mother and two brothers . . . I lived through the 1905 massacre in Odessa . . . and still remember the horror of those days as if it was yesterday." Another Russian immigrant recalled attacks by Cossacks, "pil-

Immigrants arriving in New York Harbor.

fering, killing, raping. We would hide in cellars, but it was no escaping them . . . My sister, 19 . . . said she would die rather than submit to rape." A man of Greek origins told of fleeing Ataturk's "bloodthirsty troops," who "set the city of Smyrna afire and then they started butchering everyone. . . . You Americans can never know how we . . . felt when we, in the early hours of a very cold January morning, saw you, the Statue of Liberty." Finally, a woman who had spent "many years in concentration camp by Hitler" told of having given up all hope. "I lost father, mother, 3 sister, and 2 brothers . . . Was agony, hunger, torture . . . Our uncle in the U.S. made affidavit and we arrived in 1948, January. Was a blizzard, and we pointed to that lovely Lady, the Statue of Liberty, the biggest Dream I ever had."[4]

Although millions of letters arrived, most contained modest sums; the lion's share of the money to fund Liberty's restoration came from large corporations, which financed about 90 percent of the project's $70-million cost. Some donated money outright, but most did so in exchange for permission to affix the centennial's imprimatur to their products, to call their beverage or car or umbrella ("Every time it rains, you'll remember her 100th birthday") the "official" one of Liberty's centennial. Other companies negotiated arrangements in which every time a consumer used or purchased their product, Iacocca's foundation received a tiny percentage. The best-known such tie-in was American Express's agreement to donate one penny to the restoration for each use of its credit card during the last quarter of 1983. This arrangement netted $1.7 million for the foundation; it also increased purchases with the card by 30 percent during this period. It was a good deal all around, but especially for American Express, a company just beginning to take advantage of what Madison Avenue called "cause-related marketing."[5]

Iacocca took a great deal of criticism for what some called the "commercialization of the Statue of Liberty," but his foundation, though liberal in accepting such corporate connections, didn't accept them all. His executives rejected a proposal by Seagram's to donate twenty-five cents for each of its whiskeys and wines consumed at designated bars on "official" Statue of Liberty nights. The foundation didn't want to be accused of fostering public drunkenness, even for such a patriotic cause. It also rejected requests for "official" Statue of Liberty coffins, toilet paper, and many other products deemed inappropriate. Iacocca's organization doubtless would have said no to the "Statue of Liberty Freedom Classic Thong," which showed Lady Liberty breaking the chains of sexual inhibition and promised to "cover sweet spots without covering your assets." Still, the foundation granted official status to more than a thousand items, ranging from T-shirts to tricycles, swizzle sticks to snuff boxes, potato chips to paper napkins. To add to its coffers, Iacocca's foundation turned scrap metal from the statue's rejuvenated innards into relics selling for between $10 and $300 apiece. Souvenir hunters, advertisements declared, could "have a piece of the actual lady," while tinkerers could "Build your own State of Liberty" with a kit selling for $7.95. Anyone could buy replicas large and small, of metal or Styrofoam, priced for every budget. The statue's image may have been sold almost at will, but, unlike the 1880s, the fundraising efforts proved an overwhelming success. Iacocca amassed enough money not only to pay for Liberty's makeover, but to finance a $30-million centennial celebration and, some years later, the restoration of Ellis Island.

Although French architects and engineers had been pushed aside early in the process, it was they who had successfully diagnosed many of the problems that the American architects and engineers would fix. One key issue involved the statue's head and shoulder, which engineers found to be tilted off-center—the head by about two feet and the torch-bearing shoulder by eighteen inches. As a result, one of the crown spokes touched the arm, and the shoulder was dangerously weak. The torch wasn't about to come crashing down on its own, but the restoration team decided to prevent it from deteriorating further. As for the torch's flame, it had to be removed and re-created from scratch. In 1916 Gutzon Borglum, the future sculptor of Mount Rushmore, attempted to light the flame from the inside by cutting 250 openings and installing panes of amber glass, many of them inadequately sealed. Over time, rainwater seeped in, and the flame became badly corroded.

After workmen took the entire torch down, the restoration team faced the question of how to rebuild the flame. Should they model it after the one they now had in their workshop, the flame in the form Borglum had left it, or should they re-create Bartholdi's original? If the latter, how would they know what it had looked like or exactly how it had been built? Restorers scoured French and American archives for written evidence about the design and production of the original flame but had little success. Fortunately, they did find high-quality close-up photographs of Bartholdi's monument, and these pictures showed enough detail to convince restoration officials to re-create the Frenchman's original design. Inevitably, the new version would differ from the old, but who would be able to tell?

While redoing the flame, artisans repaired the torch and arm and completely rebuilt the upper balustrade, a studio replica of which Hitchcock had used for the final terrifying scenes of *Saboteur*. Although computers helped prepare the designs, the actual work had to be done by hand. The restoration team found a group of twelve French craftsmen skilled in the nineteenth-century techniques of repoussé metalwork, the process of molding thin copper plates by delicately hammering them into shape. These artisans were invited to New York, where they re-created Bartholdi's flame, including a magnificent gilding job that, later in the process, would finally fulfill the unrealized dream of lighting Liberty's torch.

Meanwhile, restorers turned to a great many other tasks, the most crucial of which was the repair of the statue's badly corroded iron skeleton. As French engineers had suspected and Americans then confirmed, without serious structural work the Statue of Liberty would, before long, begin to sag and then lose its distinctive shape. Eventually, it would collapse altogether.

As we've seen, the skeleton has three main parts: a central pylon, or tower, that bears most of the weight; a secondary support system that links the tower to the statue's copper skin via a springlike system that transfers wind pressure from the weak copper envelope to the strong secondary and primary supports; and a grid-work of thin rectangular bars, bent to conform to the folds of the skin, that brace it from the inside and maintain its shape. The first and second parts of the skeleton had remained largely intact, but the third part, the armature of narrow iron bars, required urgent attention.

Eiffel had attached the iron bars to the inside of the skin by wrapping U-shaped copper straps around them and riveting the straps to the bars and the skin at both ends of the U. This ingenious method of attachment allowed for some give inside the U (called a "saddle"); it allowed, that is, for the skin and iron braces to move independently of each other as changing temperatures made them expand and contract. This system enhanced the structure's flexibility and prevented the skeleton from damaging the skin as each responded differently to temperature change. The problem, as Eiffel understood, is that when copper and iron touch, they produce a chemical reaction that corrodes the iron, causing it to lose strength. Eiffel tried to prevent the reaction by inserting a layer of asbestos between the two metals. But asbestos doesn't last forever, and as it gradually wore thin, the iron corroded. The French engineer's efforts thus created two problems instead of one: damaged metal and remnants of asbestos, a highly carcinogenic material.

Since corrosion makes iron swell, the damaged iron bars expanded into the space between them and the copper saddles, creating new points of corrosive contact between the two metals and eliminating the give between them. This process further weakened the iron, while exerting pressure on the saddles and the skin and eventually on the rivets that held them together. Thousands of rivets popped out of the structure, creating holes where they once had been inserted. It was as if some malign force had perforated the Statue of Liberty with a huge ice pick. Now, rainwater dripped inexorably in, and the flow of moisture accelerated the corrosion process, ensuring a vicious cycle of auto-destruction. Saddles came lose, iron bars weakened, rivets popped out or sheared off, and pressure built against the skin instead of being transferred to the skeleton's strong inner core. In time, the monument would have sagged, and sections of its copper skin would have turned into a great many hanging chads.

Another major issue concerned access to the monument and the staircase inside. Bartholdi had not planned on having visitors enter the statue and climb to the top. As a result, he had allowed for only a makeshift entrance, a roughly finished interior, and just a narrow wooden staircase for maintenance workers toiling inside. Nevertheless, from the day the statue opened, people wanted to explore its innards and look at New York Harbor from its crown. After Liberty became a national monument in 1924 the federal government made various stopgap improvements to its interior, but by 1984 the staircase had deteriorated badly and needed to be replaced.

Beyond these structural problems were the indignities that Liberty had long suffered in silence: graffiti on the underside—and even the surface—of her skin; birds' nests hidden in its folds; ugly stains on her robes; and bird droppings encrusted everywhere. Although the statue looked intact when viewed from afar, close-up inspection revealed a variety of blemishes—cracks in the right eye, lips, and chin; a damaged nostril; missing hair; and foot chains completely detached from the structure. Bartholdi had deemphasized the symbols of bondage when he turned his original sketches into a fully realized model; a century later, Liberty's trampled foot chains had become prominent once again.

Throughout the long process of analyzing the statue's damages and deficiencies, the engineers and architects involved always had to be mindful of what it means to restore a historical structure. They constantly asked themselves whether, and to what extent, Bartholdi and Eiffel's original design, methods, and materials should be reproduced. Was the goal merely to repair the ravages of time and the elements, while changing as little as possible? Or was it to create an updated Statue of Liberty, one whose structure and form would benefit from modern knowledge, technology, and techniques? To their credit, members of the restoration team addressed these questions by doing a huge amount of historical research. But in many cases they found it impossible to uncover Bartholdi and Eiffel's original conceptions and methods. And when they did succeed in discovering them, they sometimes found that the original statue, as constructed, departed in significant ways from one or both men's intentions. For example, Eiffel seems to have planned to brace the torch-bearing shoulder properly from an engineering point of view. But during construction in Paris, Bartholdi apparently changed those plans, weakening the structure and tilting the torch too close to the head, which itself was tilted and inadequately braced to the main pylon that held up the whole monument. The restoration team ardently debated whether to revert to Eiffel's design or to maintain the structure as built. The first would have automatically produced a stronger shoulder, but what if Bartholdi had had artistic reasons for altering Eiffel's design? In that case, shouldn't the restoration respect the artist's realization rather than the engineer's plans—even at the cost of complicating the structural problem at hand? Questions such as these were far from easy to sort out, especially under the pressure of finishing the project in time for the centennial celebration on the Fourth of July weekend 1986.

As restoration team members waded through these questions, they needed to get the work under way. The first task was to build elaborate scaffolding to encase the statue, scaffolding that would allow workmen to do their jobs while keeping the monument from being scratched, chipped, or dented in the strong New York Harbor winds. Bartholdi had erected the Statue of Liberty without the benefit of a scaffold, precisely because of those winds. The restoration thus needed unusually stable scaffolding that could pass the most arduous of weather tests. In September 1985, just such a test occurred when Hurricane Gloria swept through the harbor. The storm packed gale winds of seventy-three miles per hour, which buffeted the statue and its scaffolding for hours. Liberty came through unscathed.

Fortunately only a single hurricane hit during the restoration process, but workmen had to contend regularly with the rain. The constant moisture required scaffolding built of aluminum, not, as usual, of steel. The inevitable rust from the ferrous metal would have dripped onto the statue, potentially discoloring it for good. This special, custom-made scaffolding took four months to erect and cost $2 million. It was a dangerous, difficult job made more arduous by the harsh winter of 1985, though teams of builders found motivation in a competition to be the first to kiss Liberty on the lips.

When complete, the scaffolding soared three hundred feet above Liberty Island and shrouded the green goddess in a silver metal glow. Workers reported that as the winds blew through the aluminum structure it chimed, as if singing to them. The view from the top was so spectacular that restoration leaders considered building an outside elevator in which tourists could ascend to the summit of the scaffolding and observe the restoration close-up. When an elevator appeared perilous and impractical, they consulted a Ferris wheel company to see what it could do. In the end, restoration leaders dropped the idea as too dangerous and expensive.

The scaffolding enabled restoration leaders to inspect the statue's surface closely and to inventory the damage it had endured, damage that was far from trivial. But they also gained new respect for copper's ability to shield itself. Liberty's coating had remained in relatively good shape thanks to the process of patination, in which red copper turns green when exposed to moisture and air. The green patina provides a thin protective layer that keeps the metal from corroding and enables it to endure. When first erected in Paris, the statue displayed a red-brown hue, not unlike a newly minted penny. It had turned fully brown by the time of its inauguration in October 1886, and Bartholdi thought it would settle into a bronze color and look like the classical statues that had inspired him. But of course Liberty evolved naturally into the green hue we know, and the restorers took great pains to leave that patina intact.

Still, some nasty stains had to be removed—not only the ones from bird droppings, but from coal tar, incinerator smoke, and paint. Black tar designed to protect the underside of the skin had seeped through the seams of the copper plates and onto the outside of the statue. Part of Liberty's back had turned black from exposure to the island's trash incinerator, and dark paint had splashed from the torch balcony onto the statue's arm. After considering several chemical cleaners, restoration experts decided to bathe the structure with a powerful pressure-wash. That took care of most of the problems, but the cleaning effort itself caused new ones. Parts of the statue turned blue when an abrasive powder used to clean the underside of the skin leaked through the seams and mixed with rainwater. The resulting chemical reaction produced bright blue crystals of sodium bicarbonate that threatened to dissolve entire sections of the statue's green patina and give it blue polka dots. The monument had to undergo another intense power wash.

The bright aluminum scaffolding gave the external work drama and visibility, but what went on inside proved far more important. That work would enable the statue to last long enough to celebrate its bicentennial in 2086. To shore up the envelope of copper that gave Liberty her form required the replacement of its entire tertiary structure. That meant removing and then duplicating, one by one, all 1,825 individually shaped iron bars, 325 springs, 2,000 saddles (copper attachment straps), and 12,000 rivets. To prevent the copper skin from being damaged or distorted, this massive job had to be done one small section at a time, each in twenty-five painstaking steps. But to keep to the planned completion schedule, work had to proceed uninterrupted, twenty-four hours a day, such that no part of the monument remained unbraced for more than a day and a half.

At maximum speed, workers could replace 70 of the 1,825 bars each week.

Although some preservationists wanted to make the new skin support system an exact copy of the old, restoration leaders rejected the idea on grounds that the original system had failed to last even a hundred years. They decided to replace the rusting iron bars with replicas made of stainless steel 316L, a strong metal that resists corrosion. To attempt to ward off corrosion altogether, workmen coated the stainless steel bars with Teflon tape backed with pressure-sensitive silicone. The new saddles, like the old, were made of copper, and each rivet had to be "prepatinized" to prevent the restored statue from being pocked for years with red copper dots. This intricate work had to be done mainly by hand, which required a large number of highly skilled craftsmen.

Laboring on the inside involved fewer dangers and less discomfort than on the outside, with one exception: removing the asbestos. Those assigned that task had to don "spacesuits" to protect them from inhaling particles of the old insulation. During this stage of the process the Statue of Liberty looked more like an orbiting space station than a venerable American monument. The asbestos removal necessarily proceeded slowly and deliberately, and for that reason added considerably to the restoration's already soaring costs. To offset them, Iacocca's organization decided to sell Liberty's corroded old iron bars as souvenirs.

With the skin support system redone, the inner structural work neared its end. The principal remaining task was to shore up Liberty's rickety right shoulder. Engineers wanted to replace the shoulder by adapting Eiffel's original engineering design but found themselves overruled by the strict preservationists on the restoration team. The latter resolved to maintain Bartholdi's tilted torch, albeit strengthened by modern building techniques. Once the shoulder had been reinforced, restorers completed the interior work by strengthening the statue's ties to its pedestal, repairing minor damage to the girders, fixing the supports for Liberty's head, and blasting away layers of lead-based paint and the old coal tar used for waterproofing Liberty's insides. As we've seen, workers sprayed the tar with sodium bicarbonate, the main ingredient of Alka-Seltzer. The bright blue crystals that leaked through to the statue's surface must have created a fair amount of indigestion among those who saw it close up. As for the leaden paint, it succumbed to icy blasts of liquid nitrogen, a substance that clocks in at –320 degrees Fahrenheit and makes petrified paint fall to the ground.

With the statue's interior cleaned and strengthened, the restoration team now made it more accessible to tourists, who would enter the structure through two huge wooden doors, a grand new opening designed to acknowledge the public's long-held desire to go inside. For those content to climb only to the top of the pedestal, a new glass-walled elevator would enable them to do so without burning a single extra calorie. En route they could look out and up to glimpse Eiffel's elegant interior design. For tourists who wanted to experience the Statue of Liberty as a whole, the restoration team decided to build a new dual metal stairway, one side for the ascent and one for the return trip down. Once the project was complete, it would be easier to climb to the crown, although not *that* easy. It was still a matter of 354 steps, or twenty-two stories, and, to make room for two staircases, each had to be winding and narrow, with steps only a few inches across.

At the top, inside the crown, those who had braved the climb would no longer have to peer out through clouded, dirty portholes. The restoration installed clear, pristine windows, cleanable from the inside. The summit would be a prime romantic spot were it not for the Park Service rangers permanently installed there as guides and chaperones. Still, when VIP guests have been allowed up on their own, security cameras have captured plenty of intimate moments.[6]

For visitors falling ill or who are prone to acrophobia (fear of heights) or bathmophobia (fear of stairs), restoration workers installed a tiny emergency elevator to enable Park Service rangers to ascend quickly all the way to Liberty's neck and then spirit people out. Previously rangers had to evacuate the stairway, climb up to the affected person, and use a hammocklike stretcher slung over the bannister to lower the individual to the ground. This seems hardly the best way to minister to tourists overcome by a fear of heights.

The restoration's final touch was to light the Statue of Liberty as she'd never been lit before. Preservationists knew that Bartholdi had intended his statue to be a figurative beacon of liberty, not an actual lighthouse for boats. Still, it has always seemed to Americans that the monument should be lit, even if its illumination had long proved impossible to achieve. In 1986, thanks to new technology and the ingenious placement of lighting pits on Liberty Island and projectors on the torch balcony, the statue was at long last properly lit. The new techniques appeared to set the gilded flame afire while bathing the statue as a whole in an inspired crescendo of light. Liberty glows softly at her base, brighter at the hem of her robe, and still brighter at her shoulders and neck. Her illumination draws the eye ever upward until we fix our gaze on the fiery crown and torch. The Statue of Liberty has become the beacon it was destined to be.

The Centennial Celebration

A dramatic lighting ceremony opened "Liberty Weekend," the Hollywood-style extravaganza for the Statue of Liberty's hundredth birthday. At 9:19 p.m. on Thursday, July 3, 1986, President Ronald Reagan flipped a switch that sent a laser beam toward the monument, veiled in the young, dusky night. Suddenly the Statue of Liberty flashed into sight, its radiant glow stopping millions of viewers short, whether watching on television, packed along the banks of the Hudson River, or comfortably seated at a waterfront restaurant table, reserved for $400 (almost $800 today) a head. Those who wanted a longer, even more leisurely, look rented lofts with perfect harbor views for up to $43,000 a night. For the best view of all, seafarers could float around the harbor on their boats, as some forty thousand did.

All told, about six million people came to New York to witness the Statue of Liberty's centennial celebration, nearly doubling the city's population at the time. Liberty Weekend thus proved a great boon to New York tourism, though the city spent over $4 million on security, let alone the extra cost of sanitation, traffic control, and the like. Nearly three hundred Coast Guard and police boats, seconded by a platoon of divers, patrolled the waterways, while fifteen thousand officers, all working overtime, secured the streets. The airspace around Liberty Island was closed to all craft save for the scores of police helicopters sweeping the skies.

Even more than a magnet for tourists, Liberty Weekend stood out as a huge media event. Tens of millions watched it on the ABC network, which paid $10 million for the exclusive broadcast rights. Newscasters Peter Jennings and Barbara Walters anchored the four-day-long coverage, with help from ten correspondents, one hundred thirteen cameras, twenty-three microwave links, forty-four microwave dishes, eleven mobile television coverage units, two satellites, and four hundred support people. Production costs reached $4 million, but ABC made a handsome profit: all its advertising slots sold out in advance—at $165,000 for a thirty-second commercial. By way of comparison, the 1986 Super Bowl, the year's most expensive advertising venue, with only a fraction of Liberty Weekend's advertising slots to sell, marketed its thirty-second spots at $550,000 each.

ABC doubtless helped shape the centennial celebration, but the prominent Hollywood producer David Wolper masterminded the show. Wolper was best known for producing the two most successful miniseries in television history—*Roots* (based on writer Alex Haley's family history, from its West African roots to slavery in the South) and *The Thorn Birds* (an epic soap opera based on the best-selling book by the Australian writer Colleen McCullough). Wolper had also produced the much-watched 1984 Los Angeles Olympics, with its showy opening and closing celebrations. He promised to make Liberty Weekend showier still. The Hollywood icon organized four full days of events, from Reagan's lighting ceremony to a parade of eighteen tall ships up the Hudson River, to the most extravagant fireworks display in American history.

After lighting the Statue of Liberty, the president declared, "We are the keepers of the flame of liberty; we hold it high tonight for the world to see." Following Reagan's brief remarks, Wolper turned the program over to Chief Justice Warren Burger, who naturalized, en masse, sixteen thousand immigrants, some standing on Liberty Island, the rest dispersed around the country. Via satellite link, Burger administered the oath of allegiance simultaneously to the entire group. The theme that night was immigration and citizenship, and Wolper had invited twelve "remarkable naturalized Americans" to participate: Irving Berlin, Franklin Chang-Diaz, Kenneth Clark, Hanna Holborn Gray, Bob Hope, Henry Kissinger, I. M. Pei, Itzhak Perlman, James Reston, Albert Sabin, An Wang, and Elie Wiesel.

In yet another ceremony, the twelve received the Medal of Liberty, an award Wolper had created for the occasion. It didn't go unnoticed that no natives of Italy or Ireland, and only a single woman, Hanna Holborn Gray, president of the University of Chicago, graced the platform. Moreover, the lone African American, the noted psychologist and civil rights leader Kenneth Clark, shouldn't have counted as a "naturalized American." He was born in 1914 to American parents in the then U.S.-controlled Panama Canal Zone, and this heritage made him a natural, not a naturalized, American.[1] New York mayor Ed Koch tried to remedy these deficiencies by naming eighty-seven medalists of his own. But it didn't help that he had called the selection of the official twelve "idiotic."

One problematic part of the Statue of Liberty's immigration symbolism had always been the question of who should be recognized among those who had immigrated to the United States—elites or ordinary people, Europeans or those from other parts of the world. This question had become especially acute by the mid-1980s, when the overwhelming majority of recent immigrants had come from Asia and Latin America and found no particular welcome in the

Statue of Liberty. And what about African Americans, most of whom had arrived involuntarily and whose bondage mocked the freedom for which Bartholdi's monument would stand? Although few commentators noted it at the time, Clark's inclusion among Wolper's twelve inadvertently highlighted the ambiguous immigration heritage of African Americans and the paucity of African immigrants to the United States after the end of the slave trade in 1807. Black residents of the United States became American citizens in 1867 thanks to the Fourteenth Amendment, but very few Africans came voluntarily to this country between 1867 and 1924, when the Immigration Act essentially barred African immigration altogether. Since the law's repeal in 1965, growing numbers of Africans have come to this country, but the 2000 census recorded only 318,000 people who had been born in Africa and naturalized as U.S. citizens.[2] The number in 1986 would have been substantially lower—hence the embrace of Clark as a "naturalized American."

During Liberty Weekend, black Americans voiced ambivalent and conflicting reactions to the festivities. Thelma Guidry, who attended the Afro-Caribbean Cultural Festival instead of the centennial celebration, told a *Chicago Tribune* reporter, "I did not participate in the Liberty thing because I don't think that black people have the freedom, the justice that the Statue of Liberty stands for." Another young African American thought he would have that reaction as well but didn't. "I had not planned to take part in the Statue of Liberty's centennial celebration," he told *Newsday*. "I didn't, or couldn't, see how it applied to a young black man like myself. But as I rode the ferry during the early morning hours on the 4th, I looked into the face of that grand lady. And over the course of the weekend my thoughts were of how she had affected me personally. However, it wasn't until the closing ceremonies that her meaning hit me. There was nothing I could do but cry. Now I, too, am in love with The Lady."[3]

Part of what evoked that love, or at least awe, was the spectacular fireworks display Wolper orchestrated for Independence Day. Just after dark, Wolper's pyrotechnics impresario, Tommy Walker, unleashed twenty tons of fireworks from forty-two barges strategically arrayed around Liberty Island. Walker's forty thousand projectiles, all synchronized by computer with familiar musical scores, put previous Fourth of July efforts to shame. For many, this was the highlight of the weekend, which should perhaps have ended there. But Wolper was nothing if not ambitious, and two action-packed days remained. Saturday morning, July 5, began quietly enough, as First Lady Nancy Reagan reopened Liberty Island to visitors (it had been closed during the restoration) by leading a group of French and American schoolchildren to the site. Many had earned the honor by writing a winning essay about the meaning of liberty. "When the French gave the Statue of Liberty to America," wrote nine-year-old David McAdam, "we were so happy to see it! But the French were very sad to see it leave France. We made them a little one and you can see it when you visit France."[4]

Once the First Lady left the island, the problems began. Visitors had started lining up for the ferry early that morning, and the wait typically lasted five hours or more. Only so many people are allowed on the island at any one time, and considerably fewer in the statue itself. What the Park Service failed to foresee was that once on the island—or inside the monument—visitors would want to linger, reluctant to let the statue go. With so many people staying so long, huge bottlenecks inevitably ensued, both at the dock in Battery Park and outside the statue itself. Visitors waited and waited and waited—at every stage of the trip. Finally, at 3 p.m., the Park Service suspended ferry shuttles to the island and told people who had just arrived that they would have to return to Manhattan without seeing the main attraction. A dozen furious tourists staged an impromptu sit-down strike and refused to reboard the boat until they got to see the statue. The rangers relented and gave the protesters an abbreviated tour.[5]

To avoid Saturday's waits, people began queuing for the ferry to Liberty Island at 4 a.m. on Sunday. But as the day progressed the same bottlenecks occurred, with delays made that much worse by record-breaking ninety-eight-degree temperatures. Children sobbed and parents fumed. Those who made it inside the statue found their climb to the top more like a crawl. Worse, the gift shop quickly ran out of the choicest souvenirs. When asked about the situation, David Moffitt, the superintendent of Liberty Island, said, "I guess we did too good of a job making it interesting."[6]

Those who never made it to Liberty Island could at least get home, or to their hotels, in time for Wolper's closing ceremony. The hardiest souls went to watch it in person at New Jersey's Giants Stadium. But ticket prices were steep, and 15 percent of the seats remained unsold. Wolper attributed the disappointing turnout to "the fear of terrorism," but ABC remained unconcerned; commercials paid for the show many times over. The network had hired Wolper to create a spectacle at once gaudy and grandiose; he didn't disappoint. He built a twenty-tier stage complete with laser lighting, waterfalls, and a twelve-thousand-member cast. His two choruses alone numbered over one thousand, not to mention the three hundred banjo and fiddle players, the eight-hundred-and-fifty-member drill team, three hundred Jazzercize dancers, two hundred square dancers, and three hundred tap dancers. For all that, the highlight was doubtless the two hundred Elvis impersonators, most of whom looked authentic enough. Observers may have wondered what Elvis had to do with the Statue of Liberty, but Yakov Smirnoff, the Russian-born comedian, found a droll connection between the two: "People told me about Ellis Island. I thought it was Elvis Island—so I showed up wearing blue suede shoes."[7]

Still, many found the extravaganza "breathtaking," "spectacular," and "a night to remember," even if the blasé labeled it "the half-time show that would not end."[8] As for the program—and the weekend's—rationale, namely the restored and brilliantly illuminated Statue of Liberty, dissenters were few and far between. Even those upset over having to wait in line mostly used words like "awe-inspiring" and "moving" to express their feelings about the great American symbol. Beginning with Liberty Weekend, when many more people visited the monument than expected, the country seemed to experience a "Liberty Fever," as one park ranger called it, and visits to the statue continued at an unprecedented pace. During the four months following the monument's reopening on July 5, 1986, Liberty Island received the same number of visitors (1.5 million) as it did during the entire previous year. "Oh sure, we expected more people to come this year, but no one could have predicted this," Bill DeHart, the chief ranger at the statue, told *Newsday*. "I mean, it just hasn't stopped. Even after the summer ended, it didn't stop."[9]

The statue's popularity didn't seem to rub off on President Reagan and the Republican Party, which lost the Senate four months after Liberty Weekend. But Iacocca, who had directed the restoration and the centennial celebration, emerged as a public hero. The University of Pennsylvania asked candidates applying for admission in fall 1986 to name the individual with whom they'd most like to spend an evening. Among the responses, God came in first, Jesus second, and Iacocca third.[10] The former Chrysler chairman had been credited with rescuing the automobile company from bankruptcy, and now he seemed to have saved America's most precious monument, a national icon unlike any other. Leading Democrats began to see him as a top presidential contender, and a national poll conducted by the *Washington Post* and *ABC News* ranked him the third most popular Democratic candidate after Senator Gary Hart and New York governor Mario Cuomo.[11] Meanwhile, the Reagan administration had come to resent Iacocca's stature, enhanced as it was by his relentless self-promotion. Shortly before Liberty Weekend, Reagan's secretary of the interior, Donald P. Hodel, fired Iacocca as chair of the government's Statue of Liberty–Ellis Island Commission (he remained head of the corresponding, and far more important, private foundation). And the president's chief of staff, Donald Regan, reportedly disliked the auto executive so much that he refused to ride in Chrysler cars.[12] They needn't have worried. None of the three leading Democratic contenders in 1986 received the nomination two years later, and Reagan's vice-president, George H. W. Bush, succeeded him in the Oval Office, winning a landslide victory over Massachusetts governor Michael Dukakis.

If Iacocca's stature failed to endure, the Statue of Liberty's continued to grow. Despite the often kitschy, even vulgar, commercialization and the tacky souvenirs, over-the-top TV specials, and circus-style entertainment, Bartholdi's monument retained its dignity through it all—just as it always had. Long exploited by Madison Avenue, Hollywood, video gamers, politicians, cartoonists, and many others, Liberty never became a mere trademark for some product, company, or concern. The Liberty Mutual Insurance Company long ago made the Statue of Liberty its emblem, but no one identifies the statue with that company; rather, it's the other way around. Although the Statue of Liberty's meaning has evolved from one generation to the next, it has regularly eluded any particularistic grasp. The statue has meant many different things, but its significant meanings have always shaken off its trivial ones. Why this is so isn't easy to say.

Paul Goldberger, then the architecture critic for the *New York Times*, tried to explain Liberty's ability to "transcend the trivial," its refusal to "crumble into cliché," by pointing to its placement in New York Harbor, perched on an island of its own, where it perpetually performs a "gesture of welcoming." "The Statue of Liberty," Goldberger wrote, "turns the harbor into a door; it makes the place where the sea becomes New York Bay an entry, not just a body of water, and it makes the city itself, not to mention the nation that lies to its west, seem more tangible, more understandable, more coherent as a place." It helps, Goldberger added, that it's a fine piece of sculpture that sits atop an even finer piece of architecture, but most fundamentally, he wrote, it's a monument to and about the city of New York. "This great figure standing at the edge pulls New York together [and gives] the city an anchor more powerful, in its way, than the Empire State Building. The city that is too large and too busy to stop for anyone seems, through this statue, to stop for everyone."[13]

There is doubtless a great deal of truth in what Goldberger wrote, but the *New York Times* writer is too parochially New York. If the Statue of Liberty were mainly a monument to that great city, anchoring and defining it as the architecture critic says, it wouldn't enjoy such near-universal appeal. People come to visit it from all over the world not just because it represents New York—which, of course, it does—or even the United States, but because it stands for things far more universal than any one city or country, no matter how important they are. The Statue of Liberty stands for freedom and hope, both of which the United States has offered, however unevenly, to a vast number of people. But for those who can't, or won't, leave home, the statue represents aspirations that could, in theory, be realized anywhere. The statue seems infinitely adaptable, capable of inspiring people after a brief glance at pictures of it or thinking about what it might mean.

That's why replicas or facsimiles of Bartholdi's sculpture exist in thirty-five different countries, including thirteen sprinkled throughout France, four in Japan, two in the United Kingdom, and one each in nations as diverse as China, Ukraine, Kosovo, and Brazil.[14] Soon, there will be a dozen more. An enterprising French art dealer, Guillaume Duhamel, obtained permission to make twelve exact replicas of the statue using the 9.4-foot plaster model Bartholdi sculpted in 1878. The piece, donated by the artist's wife, has stood for a century in France's Conservatoire des arts et métiers, a museum of industrial design and technology. Until now, the government-run Conservatoire hasn't allowed anyone to make a mold from this plaster model for fear of damaging it. But new digital scanning methods satisfied museum officials that Duhamel could create his mold for casting in bronze without touching the model. The art dealer donated one replica to the Conservatoire, which has already installed it in its spacious courtyard, and then priced the other eleven at $1.1 million each. He quickly sold two, with the caveat that purchasers had to agree to respect the values the statue represents. "You don't want Al Qaeda buying one," Duhamel explained.[15]

It's unclear whether the Las Vegas casino New York-New York, which placed an unrelated Liberty replica on its roof, would have been allowed to buy one of Duhamel's copies. Had the casino done so, it would have spared the U.S. Postal Service a measure of embarrassment. In April 2011, a sharp-eyed philatelist noticed that a new "Forever" stamp showed not the real Statue of Liberty but the slightly distorted visage of the one designed to lure gamblers to the blackjack tables and slot machines below its feet.[16] The faces on Duhamel's models are identical to the genuine article on Liberty Island, if smaller by a factor of sixteen.

The prodemocracy Chinese students who occupied Tiananmen Square in 1989 would have qualified for a Duhamel replica, but the art dealer didn't have street protesters in mind. The young man who conceived the idea of erecting a "goddess of democracy" in Beijing had first fashioned a small model of the Statue of Liberty in his provincial hometown. He drew inspiration from postcards of the monument that friends had sent. His model proved so popular with fellow students that he decided to take it by train to Beijing, where he proposed to construct a much larger version. The unnamed student told Ellen Pall of the *New Yorker* that he wanted to sculpt "an exact replica, which . . . would have been a more powerful symbol [than the goddess ultimately built], but it would have given the government an excuse to put down the demonstration, because, although I think of the Statue of Liberty as universal, they could have said it was Western."[17] Instead, he led about thirty art students and artisans in creating their own Chinese version of the Statue of Liberty, a thirty-three-foot-high sculpture of plaster and papier-mâché. It stood for five days in Tiananmen Square directly opposite a huge portrait of Chairman Mao, confronting the Great Leader face to face. Although inspired by American democracy, the Tiananmen goddess, together with the student who stood fast in front of an armed and moving tank, came to represent a particularly Chinese understanding of the universal aspiration for liberty that Bartholdi had wanted to express.

At about the same time that the Tiananmen students made a Statue of Liberty the symbol of their aspirations for democracy, the meaning of the original in New York Harbor shifted back toward liberty as well. With the restoration of Ellis Island, completed in 1990, much of the imagery of immigration moved from Bartholdi's monument to the renovated Ellis Island building where so many millions of immigrants had been examined, "processed," and released into a new American life. The processing center has become a magnificent new museum, and the descendants of a great many immigrants have had their ancestors' names engraved on a Wall of Honor built to commemorate them. The memory of European immigration has thus taken up residence on Ellis Island, but this memory became fixed there long after our own contemporary discussion of immigration ceased to focus on New York Harbor, where no more than a trickle of newcomers lands nowadays. For decades, that discussion has centered on our long border with Mexico, where significant numbers of people from that country, as from Central and South

America, cross the frontier illegally every day. Some U.S. politicians and activists want to build a fence or wall along the border to keep undocumented immigrants out, while others dislike the symbolism such a wall would imply. These radically distinct points of view, plus new restrictive legislation in Arizona and other states, make today's immigration a volatile, highly charged concern. One of its effects has been to divert the heat of the immigration debate away from the Statue of Liberty. That, together with the renewed meanings attached to Ellis Island, have restored to the monument its original standing as beacon of liberty.

So, in a different way, has the tragedy of September 11. Daniel Libeskind, the Polish American architect named to oversee the reconstruction of the World Trade Center site, conceived his design for a new "Freedom Tower" with the Statue of Liberty in mind. "I was inspired by the Statue of Liberty," Libeskind said, "because I'm an immigrant myself to New York and my first experience to New York was arriving by ship [and] seeing the Statue of Liberty. . . . So to me, the Statue of Liberty is not just a symbol . . . it's a true icon." Libeskind wanted his Freedom Tower to be an icon as well, a symbol of liberty just like the statue facing it in the harbor. He decided to design "something that will be iconic in a profound sense to testify to the importance of this site. So I created a . . . symbolic element. The tower over 70 stories is really . . . a torch . . . that rises to also a very symbolic number: 1776 [feet]." That number would give the tower a meaning understandable to anyone who "looks in the skyline of New York." The year 1776, the architect added, is "a date that is the most important to me—the Declaration of Independence. That's what the Lady Liberty's holding in her hand, just, together with the torch. That's the date which declared that all people have full human rights. Not just Americans, everybody in the world deserves rights, justice."[18] For Libeskind, Freedom Tower would be a new Statue of Liberty, complete with torch, tablet, and the reference to 1776. The rebuilding of what terrorists had destroyed would emphasize that the United States stands for liberty now in the twenty-first century, just as much as it did in 1776.

Even if Libeskind's original intentions have been diluted by commercial and nationalistic ones, the building he helped to conceive remains dedicated to the "enduring spirit of freedom," as its cornerstone makes clear. When people ascend to its upper floors, they'll have an unobstructed view of the Statue of Liberty, and a great many tourists will likely visit the Freedom Tower, and the 9/11 memorial museum beneath it, just before or after sailing out to Liberty Island. The September 11 memorial, like the intense security on Liberty Island, will remind them of the terrible toll terrorism can take. But both the Freedom Tower and the reopened Statue of Liberty will testify to the resilience of New York City and to the power of liberty as a universal ideal.

Coda: 2011

It's a warm afternoon early in the fall, and I'm at the Statue of Liberty again, this time with my wife. The stairway to the crown, off-limits after the September 11 attacks, is now open, but only until the statue's 125th anniversary (October 28, 2011), when new renovations will shutter it once more. We wanted to hike to the top before then, which required reservations months in advance. The National Park Service allows only a dozen people up each hour, about two hundred a day.

Inside the statue, the security procedures are intense. Having threaded the airportlike screening at Battery Park, those headed for the crown undergo several additional checks. First, a Park Service ranger wraps our wrists with a green paper bracelet like those issued at amusement parks and state fairs. She then peruses our picture IDs. She's amazed we're from New York; locals rarely make the climb— or even visit Liberty Island itself—although this may change as the 125th anniversary nears. New Yorkers glimpse the Statue of Liberty from a distance all the time, but you really need to see it close up and from the inside.

In any case, the park rangers are immovably strict: no ID, no go up. An Australian couple had only one picture ID between them; the man had left his passport back at their uptown hotel. No amount of pleading convinced the ranger to allow him inside. The couple had to race to the subway, return to their hotel to grab his documents, and speed back to Battery Park in time to make their ferry reservation an hour hence. Unfamiliar with New York's subterranean maze, the Australians took the wrong train and landed in Brooklyn. When they finally reached the ferry dock nearly an hour late, they saw that no one notices your reservation time and that they needn't have rushed.

Once we pass the ID check, we're ushered into a locker room, where we're told to strip ourselves of everything but a camera and the clothes on our backs. To rent a locker, I stick my thumb in a scanner. When we return later to reclaim our possessions, the machine will match my thumb with its recorded print. Once we've stowed wallets, Kindles, keys, and phones in the high-tech locker, we then go through a full-body scanner. If we had this kind of security at airports, no shoe-bombers would ever board planes. But, of course, the airlines would never stand for it, and neither would most of us.

The first 150 steps to the top of the pedestal are relatively easy. It's only when we enter the statue itself that the staircase narrows to the width of one good-size human body. One staircase goes up and another down. Claustrophobes beware. Liberty's 354 steps wind tightly around its twenty-two-story central pylon; climbing them jacks my heartbeat to an aerobic rate. The lighting inside is dim, but there's nothing dangerous about the ascent. After ten minutes or so, the stairwell brightens; I'm approaching the top. The summit itself is tiny, with room for a half-dozen people. It's a glorious, sunny day, and the view is spectacular. Pointing to Brooklyn, the Australian asks, "Is that New Jersey?" He's completely turned about. Brooklyn is straight ahead; the graceful Verrazano-Narrows Bridge off to the right. Manhattan and the port stretch out to the left, the ghost of the World Trade Towers shadowing a skyline clipped tragically low.

The experience is nothing like what I remember of my sixth-grade trip. Then, the crown's windows were so caked with grime that I could barely see out. Replaced during the restoration, the port-holes now can be opened (with the right tools) and squeegeed clean. Everyone snaps pictures of the harbor, the torch arm up above, and the tablet below. Looking up, I remember the segment of Ken Burns's documentary showing a trio of stunt men shimmying up the rays pointing out from Liberty's crown. It seems an impossibly dangerous thing to do, but in the newsreel footage Burns had found, the skywalkers miraculously positioned themselves to wave returning doughboys home from the First World War. Refocusing on the here and now, I can see the seams of the individual copper plates that form Liberty's skin and the rivets that lock them in place. This close-up view makes me realize, again, just how ingenious Bartholdi was. He knew that both the seams and the rivets would be invisible when the statue was glimpsed from afar.

Even better than the harbor, which after all, you can see from a plane, is the underside of Liberty's copper skin. I can almost touch it in places and easily tell just how thin it is. Eiffel's brilliant engineering, updated in the 1980s restoration, is evident as well. I see exactly how the skin is laced with copper strapping, which itself is attached to thin metal arms. The only thing slightly disconcerting about being in the crown is the distinct feel of Lady Liberty swaying in the wind.

The guard lets us take our time in the crown, but after twenty minutes or so, we're ready to head down. The descent, though less arduous physically than the climb, feels uncomfortable: steep, winding, poorly lit, and narrow. The woman in front of me is so terrified that she cries audibly the whole way down. Her boyfriend has to tread dangerously backward to comfort and coax her on every step. When we finally reach the pedestal, she seems too shaken to feel much relief.

She speaks what sounds like an Eastern European language, so I can't understand what she says. But her body language is clear: she would have rather stayed on the ground. Aside from the Australian couple, most visitors aren't English-speakers. But the park rangers make precious few allowances for them. They bark orders and directions even I can't understand.

When my wife expresses sympathy for the uncomprehending visitors from abroad, one of the relatively few Americans we encounter complains that there are too many foreigners inside *our* statue. He's exercised over the number of undocumented immigrants in Sacramento, his hometown, and just doesn't like all these people in our midst who don't speak English. But the Statue of Liberty, we say, is an international wonder, the symbol of our country's openness to the world. We want foreigners to visit, no matter what tongues they speak. Our Californian holds his ground: "This is the UNITED STATES OF AMERICA," he says hotly. "They should speak ENGLISH."

When we're back at the base, we decide to end our excursion with a stop in the huge new Statue of Liberty gift shop. It's an emporium of the most wonderful kitsch: replicas of the statue from two inches to several feet tall, Liberty Barbies, flashlights in the form of the statue's torch, maple syrup in Liberty-shaped bottles, snow globes, Christmas tree ornaments, mugs, T-shirts, pens, you name it—everything "Made in China," needless to say. In one corner of the store resides a Bartholdi robot that opens and closes his mouth and eyes, moves his hands, and speaks English in a perfect Maurice Chevalier accent. It's half-serious and half-kitsch and makes a droll contrast to the excellent, if earnest, museum exhibit that occupies the statue's base. Recalling Chevalier, the Bartholdi puppet says of his creation, "Like all ladies, she only improves with age."

Coda: 2011

We'd stayed most of the day on Liberty Island and inside the great green monument. For the two of us, the total bill (not including souvenirs) came to $30, the price of a modest Manhattan lunch. The excursion to Liberty Island gets three stars in my Michelin Guide; even the most blasé of New Yorkers will find it well worth the detour.

Notes

Prologue

1. Albert Boime, *Hollow Icons: The Politics of Sculpture in 19th-Century France* (Kent, OH: Kent State University Press, 1987).
2. Quoted in ibid., 113.

ONE
The Idea

1. On and by Laboulaye, see Walter D. Gray, *Interpreting American Democracy in France: The Career of Édouard Laboulaye, 1811–1883* (Newark, DE: University of Delaware Press, 1994); Edouard Laboulaye, *Histoire politique des États-Unis: depuis les premiers essais de colonisation jusqu'à l'adoption de la constitution fédérale, 1620–1789* (Paris: Durand, 1855–66); Laboulaye, *The United States and France* (Boston: The Boston Daily Advertiser, 1862); Laboulaye, *L'état et ses limites: suivi d'essais politiques* (Paris: Charpentier, 1863); Laboulaye, *Why the North Cannot Consent to Disunion* (Edinburgh: Murray and Gibb, 1863).
2. On the intense reaction to Lincoln's assassination in France, see Hertha Pauli and E. B. Ashton, *I Lift My Lamp: The Way of a Symbol* (New York: Friedman, 1948, 1969), 7–9.
3. Frédéric Auguste Bartholdi, "The Statue of Liberty Enlightening the World," *North American Review*, 1885. On Bartholdi's pamphlet, see Pierre Provoyeur, June

Hargrove, and Catherine Hodeir, "Liberty: The French-American Statue in Art and History: An Introduction," in *Liberty: The French-American Statue in Art and History*, ed. Pierre Provoyeur and June Hargrove (hereafter Provoyeur) (New York: Harper & Row, 1986), 29.

4. Quoted in Pauli and Ashton, *I Lift My Lamp*, 38.

5. Marvin Trachtenberg, *The Statue of Liberty* (New York: Penguin, 1986), 28.

6. Pauli and Ashton, *I Lift My Lamp*, 33 (italics added).

7. Maurice Agulhon, *Marianne into Battle* (New York: Cambridge University Press, 1982).

8. Ibid.

9. Marvin Trachtenberg, *The Statue of Liberty* (New York: Penguin, 1976; revised edition, 1986), 76–77. Much of the discussion of the artistic influences on Bartholdi follows Trachtenberg's analysis in chapter 4.

10. Quoted in ibid., 26.

11. On Bartholdi's early life, see J. M. Schmitt, *Bartholdi, une certaine idée de la liberté* (Strasbourg: Editions de la nuée bleue, 1985), chapter 1; Robert Belot and Daniel Bermond, *Bartholdi* (Paris: Perrin, 2004), chapter 1.

12. Two large caches of these letters have been preserved, one in the Bartholdi museum in Colmar, the other in the manuscripts department of the New York Public Library.

13. Quoted in Belot and Bermond, *Bartholdi*, 320–21.

14. Quoted in Pierre Provoyeur, "Bartholdi and His Context," in Provoyeur, 42.

15. Trachtenberg, *Statue of Liberty*, 60: Charlotte's "hard dour features may, indeed, be recognized beneath [Liberty's] classicizing mask." See also Albert Boime, *Hollow Icons: The Politics of Sculpture in 19th-Century France* (Kent, OH: Kent State University Press, 1987), 119: "Bartholdi's liberty . . . , incorporating the features of his mother, . . . pays homage to his despoiled mother-fatherland [Alsace]."

16. Quoted in André Gschaedler, *True Light on the Statue of Liberty and Its Creator* (Narberth, PA: Livingston, 1966), 78–79.

17. On the colossal and its influence on Bartholdi, see Provoyeur, "Bartholdi and the Colossal Tradition," in Provoyeur, and Trachtenberg, *Statue of Liberty*, 42ff.

18. Quoted in Trachtenberg, *Statue of Liberty*, 46.

19. Quoted in Provoyeur, "Bartholdi and the Colossal Tradition," in Provoyeur, 71.

20. Quoted in Trachtenberg, *Statue of Liberty*, 46.

21. Belot and Bermond, *Bartholdi*, 140.

22. This part of the story is told, slightly differently in each case, in Trachtenberg, *Statue of Liberty*, chapter 2; Belot and Bermond, *Bartholdi*, chapter 6; and Provoyeur, "Artistic Problems," in Provoyeur, 88–92.

23. Denis Lacorne, *La Crise de l'identité américaine* (Paris: Gallimard, 2003), 160.

24. Jules and Edmond de Goncourt, *Journal des Goncourt: Mémoires de la vie littéraire*, (1866–70) (Paris: Charpentier, 1888), 3: 102 (January 16, 1867).

25. Alexandre Zannini, *De l'Atlantique au Mississippi, souvenirs d'un diplomate* (Paris: J. Renoult, 1884); Louis-Laurent Simonin, *A travers les Etats-Unis, de l'Atlantique au Pacifique* (Paris: Charpentier, 1875).

26. Belot and Bermond, *Bartholdi*, 232.

27. Boime, *Hollow Icons*, 118.

28. Pauli and Ashton, *I Lift My Lamp*, 59.

29. Quoted in Belot and Bermond, *Bartholdi*, 239.

30. Ibid., 242.

31. Quoted in ibid., 238.

32. Ibid., 239.

33. Boime, *Hollow Icons*, 119.

34. Provoyeur, "Artistic Problems," 92.

TWO
Paying for It

1. See for example, Robert Belot and Daniel Bermond, *Bartholdi* (Paris: Perrin, 2004), 340ff; Marvin Trachtenberg, *The Statue of Liberty* (New York: Penguin, 1976; revised edition, 1986), 181ff.

2. Quoted in Janet Headley, "Voyage of Discovery: Bartholdi's First American Visit (1871)," in *Liberty: The French-American Statue in Art and History*, ed. Pierre Provoyeur and June Hargrove (hereafter Provoyeur) (New York: Harper & Row, 1986), 100.

3. Quoted in Belot and Bermond, *Bartholdi*, 246.

4. Headley, "Voyage of Discovery," 100.

5. Edward Berenson, "American Perspectives on the French Republic," in *The French Republic: History, Values, Debates*, ed. Edward Berenson, Vincent Duclert, and Christophe Prochasson (Ithaca, NY: Cornell University Press, 2011), 360.

6. Belot and Bermond, *Bartholdi*, 245.

7. Headley, "Voyage of Discovery," 102.

8. Ibid.

9. Belot and Bermond, *Bartholdi*, 253.

10. Headley, "Voyage of Discovery," 102.

11. Ibid., 103.

12. Ibid., 104.

13. Philip M. Katz, *From Appomattox to Montmartre: Americans and the Paris Commune* (Cambridge, MA: Harvard University Press, 1998).

14. May 6, 1871, cited in ibid., 95.

15. Cited in ibid., 161.

16. On the French campaign for the Statue of Liberty, see Catherine Hodeir, "The French Campaign," in Provoyeur, 120–39; Trachtenberg, *Statue of Liberty*, 33–38; Hertha Pauli and E. B. Ashton, *I Lift My Lamp: The Way of a Symbol* (New York: Friedman, 1948, 1969), 132–49; Belot and Bermond, *Bartholdi*, chapter 13.

17. Bartholdi papers, Conservatoire national des arts et métiers (CNAM), Paris.

18. Claude Bellanger, *Histoire générale de la presse française* (Paris: PUF, 1969), 3: 221.

19. *Le Petit Journal*, September 28, 1875.

20. *Le Bien Public*, November 9, 1875; *Le Journal Illustré*, October 10, 1875. See also *Le Monde Illustré*, October 9, 1875; *L'Illustration*, October 9, 1875.

21. Quoted in Belot and Bermond, *Bartholdi*, 284.

22. Quoted in Hodeir, "French Campaign," 125.

23. *New York Times*, September 29, 1876.

24. Janet Headley, "Bartholdi's Second American Visit: The Philadelphia Exhibition (1876)," in Provoyeur, 146.

25. Hodeir, "French Campaign," 129.

26. See Vanessa Schwartz, *Spectacular Realities: Early Mass Culture in Fin-de-Siècle Paris* (Berkeley: University of California Press, 1998). See also T. J. Clark, *The Painting of Modern Life* (Princeton, NJ: Princeton University Press, 1985); Edward Berenson, *Heroes of Empire: Five Charismatic Men and the Conquest of Africa* (Berkeley: University of California Press, 2010); Gregory Shaya, "The Flaneur, the Badeau, and the Making of a Mass Public in France, Circa 1860–1910," *American Historical Review* 109 (2004). The classic nineteenth-century text on the flaneur is Charles Baudelaire, "The Painter of Modern Life," in *The Painter of Modern Life and Other Essays* (New York: Phaidon, 1995).

27. Quoted in Hodeir, "French Campaign," 129.

28. Barry Moreno, *The Statue of Liberty Encyclopedia* (New York: Simon & Schuster, 2000), 98.

29. *Le Charivari*, November 18, 1878.

THREE

Building It

1. Albert Boime, "La Statue de la liberté: une icône vide," *Le Débat* 44 (March–May 1987): 128.

2. Marvin Trachtenberg, *The Statue of Liberty* (New York: Penguin, 1976; revised edition, 1986), 127–34, provides a thorough analysis of Eiffel's skeleton.

3. Ibid., 143–44.

4. Ibid., 140.
5. Pierre Provoyeur, "Technical and Industrial Challenges," in *Liberty: The French-American Statue in Art and History*, ed. Pierre Provoyeur and June Hargrove (hereafter Provoyeur) (New York: Harper & Row, 1986), 117.
6. Ibid., 108–9.
7. Quoted in Robert Belot and Daniel Bermond, *Bartholdi* (Paris: Perrin, 2004), 361.
8. Quoted in Barry Moreno, *The Statue of Liberty Encyclopedia* (New York: Simon & Schuster, 2000), 114.
9. *Le Mouvement scientifique*, late 1884, pièce 1749, Conservatoire national des arts et métiers (CNAM), Paris.
10. André Michel, quoted in Belot and Bermond, *Bartholdi*, 344–45; *Le Quotidien*, September 11, 1884, quoted in Belot and Bermond, *Bartholdi*, 359.
11. Ibid., 360.
12. On the pedestal, see Susan R. Stein, "Richard Morris Hunt and the Pedestal," in Provoyeur, 176–85; Trachtenberg, *Statue of Liberty*, chapter 7.
13. Ibid., 143.
14. Ibid., 164.

FOUR

American Reticence?

1. Jacques Betz, *Bartholdi* (Paris: Editions de minuit, 1954); André Gschaedler, *True Light on the Statue of Liberty and Its Creator* (Narberth, PA: Livingston, 1966).
2. Hertha Pauli and E. B. Ashton, *I Lift My Lamp: The Way of a Symbol* (New York: Meredith Press, 1948; revised edition, 1969).
3. June Hargrove, "Power of the Press," in *Liberty: The French-American Statue in Art and History*, ed. Pierre Provoyeur and June Hargrove (hereafter Provoyeur) (New York: Harper & Row, 1986), 166.
4. Marcel Mauss, *The Gift: The Form and Reason for Exchange in Archaic Societies* (*Essai sur le don*) (New York: Norton, 1990). On Mauss, see Marcel Fournier's definitive intellectual biography, *Marcel Mauss, A Biography* (Princeton, NJ: Princeton University Press, 2005); Claude Levi-Strauss, *Introduction to the Work of Marcel Mauss* (London: Routledge, 1987).
5. *New York Times*, December 26, 1883.
6. Quoted in Barry Moreno, *The Statue of Liberty Encyclopedia* (New York: Simon & Schuster, 2000), 188.
7. "Le discours de M. Laboulaye," *L'Evénement*, May 1, 1876 (italics added).

8. June Hargrove, "The American Fundraising Campaign," in Provoyeur, 160, 163.

9. *Press*, October 5, 1876.

10. *San Francisco Daily Report*, July 1, 1884, quoted in Robert Belot and Daniel Bermond, *Bartholdi* (Paris: Perrin, 2004), 353.

11. *Commercial Advertiser*, October 7, 1876.

12. *New York Times*, October 3, 1882.

13. Quoted in Belot and Bermond, *Bartholdi*, 352.

14. Quoted in Pauli and Ashton, *I Lift My Lamp*, 221.

15. Hargrove, "American Fundraising," 157–58.

16. Ibid., 159.

17. Ibid.

18. "Mark Twain Aggrieved," *New York Times*, December 4, 1883.

19. *New York Times*, August 5, 1884.

20. *Frank Leslie's Illustrated Newspaper*, August 30, 1884.

21. *Life Magazine*, January 17, 1884.

22. *Evening Telegraph*, December 13, 1884.

23. Hargrove, "American Fundraising," 161.

24. Paul Starr, *The Creation of the Media: Political Origins of Modern Communications* (New York: Basic Books, 2004), 254–57. See also Thomas Ferenczi, *L'Invention du journalisme en France* (Paris: Payot, 1996).

25. Moreno, *Encyclopedia*, 190.

26. *World*, March 16, 1885.

27. *World*, August 5, 1884.

28. Quotes from Pauli and Ashton, *I Lift My Lamp*, 274–75.

29. Quoted in John Bodnar, Laura Burt, Jennifer Stinson, and Barbara Truesdell, "The Changing Face of the Statue of Liberty," unpublished paper for the National Park Service, Indiana University, Center for the Study of History and Memory, 2005, 110.

30. Ibid., 276.

31. Ibid.

32. Quoted in Pauli and Ashton, *I Lift My Lamp*, 278.

FIVE

The Unveiling

1. *Leslie's Illustrated Weekly*, May 10, 1884.

2. Lenore Skomal, *Lady Liberty: The Untold Story of the Statue of Liberty* (Kennebunkport, ME: Cider Mill Press, 2009), 127; *New York Times*, August 6, 1884.

3. FoundationsofAmerica.com; www.ascemetsection.org.

4. June Hargrove, "Reassembly on Bedloe's Island," in *Liberty: The French-American Statue in Art and History*, ed. Pierre Provoyeur and June Hargrove (hereafter Provoyeur) (New York: Harper & Row, 1986), 192.

5. *Leslie's Illustrated Weekly*, October 9, 1886, quoted in Provoyeur, 195.

6. *World*, October 26, 1886.

7. *Morning Journal*, October 29, 1886, quoted in Provoyeur, 200.

8. *Le Soleil*, November 9, 1886, quoted in Robert Belot and Daniel Bermond, *Bartholdi* (Paris: Perrin, 2004), 387.

9. Quoted in Hertha Pauli and E. B. Ashton, *I Lift My Lamp: The Way of a Symbol* (New York: Friedman, 1948, 1969), 302.

10. Quoted in Albert Boime, *Hollow Icons: The Politics of Sculpture in 19th-Century France* (Kent, OH: Kent State University Press, 1987), 134. On the Haymarket Affair, see Alan Trachtenberg, *The Incorporation of America: Culture and Society in the Gilded Age* (New York: Hill and Wang, 2007), 88–91.

11. Quoted in Boime, *Hollow Icons*, 134.

12. Trachtenberg, *Incorporation of America*, 90–91.

13. Quoted in Boime, *Hollow Icons*, 136.

14. *Cleveland Gazette*, November 27, 1886, quoted in Glassberg, "Rethinking the Statue of Liberty: Old Meanings, New Contexts," paper prepared for the National Park Service, December 2003, 4. See also Rebecca M. Joseph, with Brooke Rosenblatt and Carolyn Kinnebrew, "The Black Statue of Liberty Rumor: An Inquiry into the History and Meaning of Bartholdi's *Liberté éclairant le Monde*," unpublished report prepared for Northeast Ethnography Program, Boston Support Office, National Park Service, September 2000.

15. John Bodnar, Laura Burt, Jennifer Stinson, and Barbara Truesdell, "The Changing Face of the Statue of Liberty," unpublished paper for the National Park Service, Indiana University, Center for the Study of History and Memory, 2005, 176.

16. Quoted by Richard Wormser, www.pbs.org/wnet/jimcrow/stories_events _14th.html.

17. The Tuskegee Institute (later Tuskegee University) kept what most historians consider reliable, if conservative, annual statistics on lynching from 1892 to 1959. The *Chicago Tribune* also compiled statistics on lynching beginning in 1882. Accurate statistics do not exist for earlier years, although the numbers are thought to be high. During Reconstruction (1865–77), opponents of black enfranchisement used lynching to terrorize African Americans who dared to take advantage of their newly won rights.

18. Nell Irvin Painter, "Who Was Lynched?" *Nation* 253, no. 16 (November 11,

1991): 577; Michael J. Pfeifer, *Rough Justice: Lynching and American Society, 1874–1947* (Chicago: University of Illinois Press, 2004).

19. The classic work on Jim Crow is C. Van Woodward, *The Strange Career of Jim Crow* (New York: Oxford University Press, 1955). See also Leon F. Litwack, *Trouble in Mind: Black Southerners in the Age of Jim Crow* (New York: Knopf, 1998); Richard Wormser, *The Rise and Fall of Jim Crow* (New York: Macmillan, 2003).

20. Quoted in Bodnar, Burt, Stinson, and Truesdell, "Changing Face," 183.

21. Ibid., 185.

SIX
Huddled Masses

1. Pierre Provoyeur and June Hargrove, eds., *Liberty: The French-American Statue in Art and History* (New York: Harper & Row, 1986) (hereafter Provoyeur).

2. Data from the Economic History Association, http://eh.net/encyclopedia/article/cohn.immigration.us.

3. James Webb, *Born Fighting: How the Scots-Irish Shaped America* (New York: Broadway Books, 2004).

4. Ibid.

5. Marvin Trachtenberg, *The Statue of Liberty* (New York: Penguin, 1976; revised edition, 1986), 88.

6. Quoted in ibid., 88.

7. Quoted in ibid., 71.

8. On Windom, political cartoons, and the new immigration facility, see Roger A. Fisher, "William Windom, Cartoon Centerfold, 1881–1891," *Minnesota History Magazine* (Fall 1988): 107–8.

9. Ibid. See also Anne Cannon Palumbo and Ann Uhry Abrams, "Proliferation of the Image," in Provoyeur, 236.

10. *Judge*, March 22 and April 12, 1890.

11. "Boss Platt's Latest Outrage," *Puck*, March 19, 1890.

12. *Evening Telegram*, September 10, 1892.

13. Christian Blanchet and Bertrand Dard, *Statue of Liberty: The First Hundred Years*, trans. Bernard A. Weisberger (New York: American Heritage, 1985), 111.

14. http://xroads.virginia.edu/~cap/liberty/aldrich.html.

15. Thomas Bailey Aldrich, *Unguarded Gates and Other Poems* (Boston: Houghton Mifflin, 1895). On Aldrich, see Rudolph J. Vecoli, "The Lady and the Huddled Masses: The Statue of Liberty as a Symbol of Immigration," in *The Statue of Liberty Revisited*, ed. Wilton S. Dillon and Neil G. Kotler (Washington, DC: Smithsonian Institution Press, 1994), 49.

16. For a description of the workings of Ellis Island, see Barry Moreno, *Ellis Island* (Chicago: Arcadia, 2003); James B. Bell and Richard I. Abrams, *In Search of Liberty: The Story of the Statue of Liberty and Ellis Island* (Garden City, NY: Doubleday, 1984), 80–89.

17. All quotations in this paragraph from John Bodnar, Laura Burt, Jennifer Stinson, and Barbara Truesdell, "The Changing Face of the Statue of Liberty," unpublished paper for the National Park Service, Indiana University, Center for the Study of History and Memory, 2005.

18. Gay Talese, "Miss Liberty—Uptown," *New York Times*, October 2, 1960.

19. Quoted in Israel Zangwill, "Afterword," *The Melting Pot, Drama in Four Acts* (New York: McMillan, 1917), 199. First quotation from the play, 31; second, 184.

20. Barbara Blumberg, *Celebrating the Immigrant: An Administrative History of the Statue of Liberty National Monument, 1952–1982* (Washington, DC: National Parks Service, 1985), 10.

21. On Lazarus's Jewishness and her life and work in general, see Esther Schor, *Emma Lazarus* (New York: Schocken, 2006), esp. chapter 2.

22. Albert Boime, *Hollow Icons: The Politics of Sculpture in 19th-Century France* (Kent, OH: Kent State University Press, 1987), 137.

23. Quoted in Max Cavitch, "Emma Lazarus and the Golem of Liberty," in *The Traffic in Poems: Nineteenth-Century Poetry and Transatlantic Exchange*, ed. Meredith L. McGill (New Brunswick, NJ: Rutgers University Press, 2008), 113.

24. Quoted in Hertha Pauli and E. B. Ashton, *I Lift My Lamp: The Way of a Symbol* (New York: Friedman, 1948, 1969), 227. See also the excellent analysis in Cavitch, "Emma Lazarus," 97–122.

25. Ibid., 115.

26. O. Henry, "The Lady Higher Up," in *Sixes and Sevens* (New York: Street and Smith, 1903), 214–19.

27. *Literary Digest*, July 5, 1919 (originally published in *Memphis Commercial Appeal*).

28. *Brooklyn Eagle*, reprinted in *Literary Digest*, July 12, 1919.

29. See "History Matters," www.historymatters.gmu.edu/d/5078/.

30. Bodnar, Burt, Stinson, and Truesdell, "Changing Face," 111.

31. Quoted in ibid., 112.

32. Ibid.

33. John Higham, "Transformation of the Statue of Liberty," in *Send These to Me: Jews and Other Immigrants in Urban America* (New York: Atheneum, 1975), 78–87.

34. Quoted in Vecoli, "Lady and the Huddled Masses," 57.

35. Quoted in ibid., 56.

36. Matthew Baigell, *Jewish Art in America: An Introduction* (Lanham, MD: Rowman and Littlefield, 2007), 60.

37. Gary B. Nash, *The Liberty Bell* (New Haven: Yale University Press, 2010).

SEVEN

From Neglect to Commemoration

1. Barbara Blumberg, "A National Monument Emerges: The Statue as Park and Museum," in *Liberty: The French-American Statue in Art and History*, ed. Pierre Provoyeur and June Hargrove (hereafter Provoyeur) (New York: Harper & Row, 1986), 210.

2. Ibid., 212.

3. *New York Times Magazine*, June 22, 1941, quoted in John Higham, "Transformation of the Statue of Liberty," in *Send These to Me: Jews and Other Immigrants in Urban America* (New York: Atheneum, 1975), 79. See also the *New Yorker*, November 30, 1940.

4. Barbara Blumberg, *Celebrating the Immigrant: An Administrative History of the Statue of Liberty National Monument, 1952–1982* (Washington, DC: National Parks Service, 1985).

5. Barbara Blumberg, "A National Monument Emerges: The Statue as Park and Museum," in Provoyeur, 214.

6. Ibid.

7. Blumberg, *Celebrating the Immigrant*, 11.

8. Ibid., chapter 2.

9. Ibid., 58.

10. www.census.gov/population/www/documentation/twps0029/tab09.html.

11. Peter Novick, *That Noble Dream: The Objectivity Question and the American Historical Profession* (New York: Cambridge University Press, 1988), 366ff.

12. Blumberg, *Celebrating the Immigrant*, 63. On the "salad bowl," see George E. Pozzetta, ed., *Assimilation, Acculturation and Social Mobility* (New York: Garland, 1991).

13. Blumberg, *Celebrating the Immigrant*, 64.

14. Ibid., 65.

15. Ibid., 69.

16. Ibid., 84.

17. Ibid.

18. For a history of Ellis Island, see Ann Novotny, *Strangers at the Door: Ellis Island, Castle Garden, and the Great Migration to America* (Riverside, CT: Chatham Press, 1971).

19. Blumberg, *Celebrating the Immigrant*, 97.

20. Ibid., 98.

EIGHT
The Popular Imagination

1. Anne Cannon Palumbo and Ann Uhry Abrams, "Proliferation of the Image," in *Liberty: The French-American Statue in Art and History,* ed. Pierre Provoyeur and June Hargrove (New York: Harper & Row, 1986), 231.

2. Lyrics and stage directions from the typed copy of Green's play in National Archives and Records Administration (College Park, Md.), Record Group 69: Federal Theater Project Collection, Box 294. There is another copy in Library of Congress, Music Division, Federal Theater Project Collection, Box 684. My thanks to the distinguished musicologist Tim Carter (University of North Carolina-Chapel Hill) for this reference.

3. Palumbo and Abrams, "Proliferation," 259.

4. Ibid.

5. A Universal Studios production.

6. An MGM production.

7. This final scene, with Heston's melodramatic cry of despair, has invited a steady stream of parody, among them Mel Brooks's film *Spaceballs,* Kevin Smith's *Jay and Silent Bob Strike Back,* and in two episodes of *The Simpsons.*

8. Quoted in Barbara Blumberg, *Celebrating the Immigrant: An Administrative History of the Statue of Liberty National Monument, 1952–1982* (Washington, DC: National Parks Service, 1985), 14.

9. Most of the information presented here about the Statue of Liberty and film comes from the Internet. See, especially, the Wikipedia entry "The Statue of Liberty in Popular Culture," en.wikipedia.org/wiki/Statue_of_Liberty_in_popular_culture; "Liberty Destroyed," www.youtube.com/watch?v=cOoMC1xH5DU&NR=1; "Top Ten Movies that Feature the Statue of Liberty," www.toptenz.net/top-10-movies-that-feature-the-statue-of-liberty.php; "Miss Liberty: The Statue of Liberty in Film," www.squidoo.com/statueoflibertyinmovies.

10. Barbara A. Babcock and John J. Macaloon, "Everybody's Gal: Women, Boundaries, and Monuments," in *The Statue of Liberty revisited,* ed. Wilton S. Dillon and Neil G. Kotler (Washington, DC: Smithsonian Institution Press, 1994), 92.

11. *Village Voice,* October 26, 2004; proteinwisdom.com/?p=17390.

NINE
Restoration

1. *World,* April 19, 1885.

2. Quoted in *The Nation,* November 9, 1985.

3. Lynne Bundesen, ed., *Dear Miss Liberty* (Salt Lake City, UT: Gibbs M. Smith, 1986), 2, 41, 57.

4. Ibid., 17, 35, 42. 54.

5. The bulk of this chapter is based on Richard Seth Hayden and Thierry W. Despont's *Restoring the Statue of Liberty* (New York: McGraw Hill, 1986), the definitive work on the project. Hayden and Despont helped lead the effort, and they wrote their account of it with the aid of Nadine M. Post and the photographer Dan Cornish. For this chapter I have also drawn heavily on the many press accounts of the restoration project.

6. Richard Seth Hayden and Thierry W. Despont, with Nadine M. Post, *Restoring the Statue of Liberty: Sculpture, Structure, Symbol* (New York: McGraw Hill, 1986), 87–88.

TEN

The Centennial Celebration

1. Congressional legislation of 1937 made natural U.S. citizenship retroactive to those born in the Canal Zone after February 1904, provided they had at least one parent with U.S. citizenship.

2. www.census.gov/population/cen2000/stp-159/STP-159-africa.pdf. Recently, significant numbers of people of African ancestry from the Caribbean have been naturalized as U.S. citizens. See www.dhs.gov/xlibrary/assets/statistics/publications/NaturalizationFlowReport2004.pdf.

3. *Chicago Tribune*, July 6, 1986; *Newsday*, July 17, 1986.

4. Quoted in the *Chicago Tribune*, July 6, 1986.

5. Much of this chapter is based on a wide reading of newspaper and magazine accounts of Liberty Weekend and its aftermath. I have drawn in particular from *Newsday*, *New York Times*, *Los Angeles Times*, *Chicago Tribune*, *New York Daily News*, and *Time*.

6. *Newsday*, July 7, 1986.

7. *Ottawa Citizen*, July 7, 1986.

8. *New York Times*, July 7, 1986.

9. *Newsday*, November 10, 1986.

10. *Ottawa Citizen*, July 7, 1986.

11. Ibid.

12. Ibid.

13. *New York Times*, July 17, 1986.

14. My thanks to Carol Gluck of Columbia University for identifying the Japanese replicas, one of which is in the town of Oirase, which stands at the same latitude as New York City. See "Les Statues de la Liberté dans le monde," *Fontes* 12 (January 1994); en.wikipedia.org/wiki/Replicas_of_the_Statue_of_Liberty.

15. *New York Times,* June 9, 2011.
16. *New York Times,* April 14, 2011.
17. *New Yorker,* October 23, 1989.
18. Daniel Libeskind interviewed by the Discovery Channel, September 16, 2010, blogs.discovery.com/rebuilding-ground-zero/2010/09/statue-of-liberty-inspired -ground-zero-design.html.

Index

Page numbers in *italic* type indicate illustrations.

ABC television, 182, 186, 187

Abelman, Ida: *My Father Reminisces*, 125

abolitionism, 9, 10, 11, 23, 27, 28, 31, 32, 34, 38, 98, 104

Abrams, J. J., 156

Adamic, Louis, 123

Adjustment Bureau, The (film), 155

advertising: Liberty image use in, 2, 55, 140–45, 160, 170, 188; Liberty Weekend and, 170–71, 182

African Americans, 35, 38, 134, 157, 183, 184; American Museum of Immigration portrayal of, 135–36; Liberty Weekend and, 184; oppression of, 98–100, 104, 134

African immigrants, 134, 184

Afro-Caribbean Cultural Festival, 184

Aldrich, Thomas Bailey, 111–13; "Unguarded Gates," 112–13

Alsace, 14, 24, 25, 26–27, 38

America First, 145

American Committee, 67, 69–70, 78–79, 83, 85, 86, 91, 127

American Express, 170

American Hebrew, The (magazine), 118

Americanization, 116–17, 133, 149–50

American Museum of Immigration, 132–39

American Revolution, 10, 32; French aid to, 24, 33, 42, 43, 48, 74

Ammann & Whitney (engineers), 167
Annunzio, Frank, 136
Antiquities Act (1906), 128
anti-Semitism, 118
Arc de Triomphe, 17, 52
arm (Statue of Liberty), 28, 47–49; display of, 50, 78, 140; engineering of, 60; strengthening of, 128, 172, 178. *See also* torch
Army, U.S., 127, 129
Artificial Intelligence (film), 159
Art Loan Exhibition, 79
asbestos, 61, 173; removal of, 178
Asher, Sarah, 114–15
Ashton, E. B., 73
Asian immigrants, 121, 134, 136, 183–84; exclusion of, 87, 105
Astor, John Jacob, 75
Atlantic Monthly (magazine), 112–13
Attica Brigade, 157

Bandel, Ernst von: *Arminius*, 17, 20
Barnum, P. T., 76
Bartholdi, Charlotte (mother), 15–16, 26, 32, 67
Bartholdi, Emilie Jeanne Baheux (wife), 16, 26
Bartholdi, Frédéric Auguste, 8–29, 88, 91, 101–2, 197; America and, 26, 29, 30–37, 41–50, 69, 74, 75, 86, 94, 132;

background of, 13–16; colossal statuary and, 17–22, 27–29, 40, 70, 71; Franco-Prussian War and, 24–26, 27; French patriotism and, 38, 68–69; fund-raising and, 39, 40–41, 46, 50–56, 119; intricacy of work of, 61–62; liberal ideals of, 8, 13, 24, 25, 27; Liberty's beginnings and, 3–6, 10–11, 13–15, 27–29, 32, 33, 35, 101, 139, 180; Liberty's construction and (*see* construction); Liberty's definitive model and, 28–29, 57, 61, 83, 189–90; Liberty's French replica and, 68; Liberty's meaning and, 76–77, 98, 140, 174; Liberty's site choice and, 5, 31, 36, 41, 78; Philadelphia centennial exhibit and, 47, 49–50; works of: *The Curse of Alsace*, 26–27; *Egypt Carrying the Light to Egypt*, 22; Lafayette statue (N.Y.C.), 48, 77; *Lion of Belfort*, 27, 38; *Vercingétorix*, 38. *See also* Statue of Liberty
Bartholdi, Jean-Charles (father), 14–15
Bastille Day, 4
Batman Forever (film), 158
Battery Park, 1, 4–5, 31, 194, 195
Beattie, John, 91, 92
Bedloe's Island, 60, 70–72, 86, 90–91; Army installation at, 127, 129; as Bartholdi's site

choice, 5, 31, 36, 41, 78; congressional designation as site, 47, 69; crated, unopened statue at, 69, 89; immigration processing center at, 108, 109–11, 127; Liberty's completion at, 55, 57, 83; Liberty's fiftieth birthday event at, 123–24; Liberty's potential placement on, 44; Liberty's unveiling at, 94–95, 101; name change of (*see* Liberty Island); visitor numbers to, 131
Bennett, James Gordon, 85
Berlin, Irving, 149, 183
Bismarck, Otto von, 24, 25, 26
Blechman, Robert O.: "Over 17 Billion Served," 143, *144*
Blunt, Emily, 155
Bly, Nellie, 85
Boime, Albert, 3
Booth, Mary Louise, 32
Borglum, Gutzon, 171
Boston, 36, 78
Boy Scouts, 145
Bozérian, Jules François, 16
Braun, W. C., 100
Brazil, 189
bridge building, 58–59, 60
British immigrants, 105, 133
Brodie, William A., 91
Brooklyn Museum, 116
Burger, Warren, 183
Burns, Ken, 196
Burroughs, John, 117

Bush, George H. W., 188
Bush, George W., 163–64
Butler, Richard, 66

Cabanel, Alexandre, 56
Carnegie, Andrew, 74
Carpenter, John, 155–56
cartoons. *See* political cartoons
Castle Garden (N.Y.), 107
Catholicism, 79, 105, 106
Census, U.S., 134
centennial of American independence (1876), 10, 32, 35, 40, 41, 46–50, 76, 82; Liberty's arm and torch exhibited at, 49–50, 52, 140
centennial of Statue of Liberty (1986). *See* Liberty Weekend
Central Park (N.Y.C.), 31, 35
Cernuschi, Henri, 67
Champagne, Liberty logo and, 55, 141
Chang-Diaz, Franklin, 183
Charivari, Le (weekly), 53–54, 55
Chicago, 36, 60, 96–97, 106
Chicago Tribune, 184
China, 189, 190–91
Chinese Exclusion Act (1882), 87, 105
Chinese immigrants, 87, 105, 134
Chrysler, 167, 187, 188
citizenship, 183, 184
civil rights, 100, 101
Civil Rights Act (1875), 99
civil rights movement, 134

Civil War, American, 34, 38;
French positions on, 9–11, 13,
27, 32–33, 43; Reconstruction
era and, 28, 99
Clark, Kenneth, 183, 184
classical form. *See* neoclassicism
Cleveland, Grover, 7, 85–86, 94,
95, 96, 98
Cleveland Gazette, 98, 99
Clinton, Hilary, 165
Cloverfield (film), 156
Coke bottle, 143, *145*
Collège de France, 9
colossal statuary, 3, 4, 6, 17–22,
27, 28–29, 40, 71, 102
Colossi of Thebes, 19–20, 21
Colossus of Rhodes (Erlach), 17, *18*
Columbia image, 98
Confederacy, 32
Congress, U.S., 47, 69, 86, 127,
128, 131, 132, 133
Conservatoire des arts et métiers,
190
Constitution, U.S., 91
construction, 57–69; of arm,
47–49, 50, 60; asbestos use
and, 61, 173, 178; assemblage
of numbered pieces and, 65,
92–93; beginning of (early
1880s), 50, 56; coating and
(*see* copper plates); definitive
model for, 57, 61, 83, 189–90;
dismantling for shipment to
America of, 58, 67–68, 69, 86;
drawing of, *93*; fund-raising
for, 39–56; hazards of, 62; of

head, 52–53; main pylon and
secondary structure and,
59–61, 65 (*see also* iron skeleton); model enlargement
stages of, 60–63; mounting
costs of, 52–53; numbering
and cataloguing of pieces and,
64, 92; Paris workshop site
of, 58, 61–68; photographic
record of, 62–63, 65, 92, 172;
plaster versions of, 63; press
attention to, 64–65; shipment
to America of, 69, 88; stages
of, 57–58, 63–64; terra cotta
models and, 54–55; time
duration of, 56, 64; wood
molds and, 63–64. *See also*
foundation; pedestal
Coolidge, Calvin, 128
copper plates, 45, 58, 59–66,
196; deterioration of, 126;
hanging on frame of, 65–66,
92–93, 173, 177; iron skeleton's corrosion and, 174; as
Liberty's skin, 64; numbered
pieces of, 64, 92; patination
of, 5, 176–77; restoration of,
167, 172; support system for,
177–78; thinness of, 5
corporations, 170–71
Corsi, Edward, 125
Cowell, Simon, 160
Crespi, C. B.: St. Charles
Borromeo, 17
Croatian terrorists, 158
crown, 180; ascent to, 179, 194,

195–96; seven spokes of, 28, 44; view from, 5, 174, 179–80, 195–96

CSI NY (TV series), 160

Cuomo, Mario, 187

Currier and Ives: "Star Lamps," 141

Dalrymple, Louis, 110

Day After Tomorrow, The (film), 159

Declaration of Independence, 91. *See also* centennial of American independence

Deep Impact (film), 159

DeHart, Bill, 186

Delacroix, Eugène: *Liberty Leading the People*, 11, 12, 101–2

Democratic Party, 84–87, 137, 187, 188

Depew, Chauncey M., 96, 97, 98

De Wolf, Rose, 137

dioramas, 50–52

Doré, Gustave, 56

Drexel, Joseph W., 70, 75

DuBois, W. E. B., 100–101; *Autobiography*, 100

Duhamel, Guillaume, 189–90

Dukakis, Michael, 188

Dumoulin, R.: *Liberation*, 147

Du Pont, Pierre S., III, 132, 138–39

Ecole des beaux-arts, 13, 69, 166

Ecole polytechnique, 166

Egypt, 6, 17, 19–22; Bartholdi's Suez colossal monument proposal for, 21, 27, 28–29, 70, 71

Eiffel, Gustave, 6, 63, 92, 131, 173, 174, 175, 179, 196; innovations of, 58–60

Eiffel Tower, 6, 52, 58, 66

Eisenhower, Dwight, 138

Ellis Island, 111, 113–14, 115, 125, 168, 186, 192; closure (1954) of, 132, 138; oral histories and, 137; restoration and museum project, 138–39, 171, 191; symbolism of, 138; Wall of Honor, 191

Emerson, Ralph Waldo, 117

Emmerich, Roland, 159

Erlach, Fischer von: *Colossus of Rhodes*, 17, 18

Ernst, Robert, 135

Escape from New York (film), 155–56

Etex, Antoine, 17

ethnicity, 106, 107, 133–36, 137

Evarts, William M., 86, 95

Fairmount Park (Phila.), 35, 49, 78, 89

Fairmount Park Commission, 35

Federal Theatre Project, 149

female images. *See* women

feminism, 101

ferryboats, 5, 31, 127, 129, 131, 185–86

Fietz, Bluma Clara, 168

Figaro, Le (newspaper), 45
films, 140, 151–56, 158–59, 188
fireworks, 182, 185
First World War. *See* World
　War I
flânerie, 51
Flattau, William H., 115–16
Forney, John W., 34, 35, 40, 46,
　88
Fort Hood, 127
foundation, 7, 86, 90–91;
　appearance of, 5; enlargement
　of, 133; floodlighting of, 128;
　measurements of, 70. *See also*
　pedestal
Fourteenth Amendment, 99, 184
Franco-American Committee
　(1981), 166–67, 168, 171
Franco-American Union (1875),
　40–41, 42, 43, 46, 53; Ameri-
　can Committee of, 67, 69–70;
　French members of, 40
Franco-Prussian War, 24–27,
　33, 38, 40, 43, 45, 46, 68
*Frank Leslie's Illustrated News-
　paper*, 38–39, 90, 92; "The
　'Statue of Liberty' One
　Thousand Years Later," 81, *82*
Freedom of the City (N.Y.C.
　medal), 94
Freedom Tower, 192–93
Freemasonry, 28, 91
French Revolution of 1789, 4, 7,
　11–13, 38
French Revolution of 1830, 11,
　12, 38

French Revolution of 1848, 13,
　21, 32, 38
fund-raising, 10, 30, 35, 39–56,
　64, 133, 139; American
　problems with, 69–70, 73–89;
　French methods of, 46, 47,
　50–56, 79, 83, 119; Liberty's
　restoration and, 126, 128, 166,
　167–71; Pulitzer's small-
　donors campaign and, 6,
　84–89

Gage and Gauthier (workshop),
　61–64, 65
Galleani, Luigi, 123
Gambetta, Leon, 25
Gan, Stephen, 163
Garfield, James A., 39
Garibaldi, Giuseppe, 24
Garnier, Charles, 63
General Services Administration,
　138
Génie Civile, La (magazine),
　62–63
George, Henry, 84, 97–98,
　118–19
German immigrants, 23, 105,
　122, 133
Germany, 17, 23, 24, 33, 40, 68,
　79; Liberty sabotage and, 156;
　Nazis policies and, 124,
　130–31, 150. *See also* Franco-
　Prussian War
Ghostbusters II (film), 159
Giants' Stadium (N.J.), 186
gift-giving, psychology of, 74

GI Joe, The Movie (film), 158
goddesses of liberty, 11–12, *12*,
    13, 21
Goldberger, Paul, 188–89
Goncourt, Jules and Edmond de,
    23–24
Gould, Jay, 83, 84
Gounod, Charles: "La Liberté
    éclairant le monde," 47
Grant, Ulysses S., 23, 34, 36,
    46
Grant, Ulysses S., III, 132
Gray, Hanna Holborn, 183
Green, Paul (*Johnny Johnson*),
    145–49
Grévy, Jules, 67
Grimm, Thomas, 42–43
Guidry, Thelma, 184

hand (Statue of Liberty), 6, 28.
    See also arm
Harper's Bazaar (magazine), 32
Harper's Weekly, 44, 97
Hart, Gary, 187
Hart, Moss, 149
Haussmann, Georges-Eugène,
    51, 66
Hayes, Rutherford B., 86
Haymarket riot (1886), 96–97
head (Statue of Liberty): inad-
    equate bracing of, 175; Paris
    Exposition display of, 52, *53*,
    64; restoration and, 171, 179;
    visitors' access, 50, 58. *See also*
    crown
Heine, Heinrich, 117

Henry, O.: "The Lady Higher
    Up," 120, 159
Hewitt, Abram, 84
Hitchcock, Alfred, 151, 153, 156,
    172
Hitler, Adolf, 124, 131, 150, 169
Hodel, Donald P., 188
Holen, Olaf, 168
Hope, Bob, 183
Hudson River, 181; tall ships
    parade, 182
Hugo, Victor, 67
Hunt, Richard Morris, 69–72,
    91, 92
Hurricane Gloria, 175–76

Iacocca, Lee, 167–68, 170–71,
    178, 187–88
Iannarelli, Giuseppe, 122
illustrated press, 43–44, 50, 83,
    85
immigration, 3, 104–25, 126,
    149–50; advocates of, 117–19;
    Americanization and, 116–17,
    133, 149–50; barriers to, 87,
    108, 109, 113, 121–25, 129,
    133–34, 184, 192; contribu-
    tions to America of, 123–24,
    134, 183; ethnic stereotyping
    and, 136; Eurocentric focus
    on, 134, 188–89, 191; hostility
    toward, 108–13, 120–21, 197;
    as labor source, 104–5, 106;
    Liberty Weekend naturaliza-
    tion event and, 183; metaphors
    for, 133–35; museum projects

immigration (continued)
and, 132–39, 191; non-
Europeans and, 183–84,
191–92; open policy of, 76–77;
peak years of, 105–6, 113, 149;
refugees from Nazism and,
130–31; Statue of Liberty
symbolism and, 84, 114–15,
123–25, 129, 132, 145,
149–50, 168–69. *See also* Ellis
Island
Immigration Act (1924), 113,
121–22, 184; repeal (1965) of,
184
Immigration and Naturalization
Service, 138
Independence Day (film), 158–59
industrialization, 104–5, 106
Iranian dissidents, 157
Irish immigrants, 105–6, 120,
133, 183
iron skeleton, 6, 59–61, 65–66,
92; anchoring of, 60; asbestos
layer and, 61, 173, 178;
corrosion of, 173–74; interior
visibility of, 58; repair of,
172–73, 175; rusting of,
131; truss-work of, 59
Isère, L' (steamship), 69, 88
Ismail, khedive of Egypt, 20–22,
70
Italian immigrants, 90, 106, 121,
122, 125, 183

Janet-Lange, Ange-Louis, 13; *La
France éclarant le monde* (*France

*Illuminating [or Enlightening]
the World*), 13, *14*
Japan, 189
Japanese immigrants, 134
Jennings, Peter, 182
Jersey City (N.J.) munitions
dump sabotage, 156
Jewish immigrants, 106, 117–18,
119, 136; discrimination and,
133–34; as refugees from
Nazism, 124, 130, 169
Jim Crow laws, 100, 104, 134
Jobs Corps, 139
Johnny Johnson (Weill), 145–49,
159
Johnson, Lyndon, 139
Journal Illustré, Le, 43–44
Judge (magazine), 109–10, *141*
Julien, Claude, 67–68
July 4, 1776, 4, 28, 41, 67, 86,
143, 193; Liberty Weekend
and, 181, 185. *See also* centen-
nial of American independence
July 14, 1789, 4

Kabe, Priscilla, 151–53
Kennedy, John F., 139
Kim Il-Sung, 17
King, David H., Jr., 90, 91
Kipling, Rudyard: *Souvenirs of
France*, 52
Kissinger, Henry, 183
Koch, Ed, 183
Kosciuszko Foundation, 136
Ku Klux Klan, 99–100
Kusielewicz, Eugene, 136

L & M cigarettes, 143
labor, 104–5, 106, 113, 122, 123.
See also strikes
Laboulaye, Edouard René de, 6,
8–10, 26, 74, 76; American
contacts of, 31, 32, 34; fund-
raising and, 39–41, 43, 45–47;
Liberty's meaning to, 76–77,
98; political ideals of, 8, 13, 23,
24, 25, 28, 31, 35, 38; works
of: *History of the United States*,
8–9; *Paris in America*, 9
Lady Gaga, 162–63, 165
Lady Liberty. *See* Statue of
Liberty
Lafayette, marquis de, 8, 23, 33,
41, 42, 94; Bartholdi statue of,
48, 77
Lafayette, Oscar de, 8, 40, 41
Lagarrigue, Jean: "Miss Liberty/
Coca Cola," 143, *145*
Lasteyrie, Jules de, 40
Las Vegas New York-New York,
190
Lazarus, Emma, 6–7, 117–18,
119; *Epistles to the Hebrews*,
118; "In the Jewish Synagogue
at Newport," 117. *See also*
"New Colossus, The"
Lesbazeilles, E., 18
Leslie's Weekly. See *Frank Leslie's
Illustrated Newspaper*
Lesseps, Ferdinand de, 21, 94
liberty, 2, 3, 5, 9, 76, 77, 97,
150–51, 189, 191–93; Ameri-
cans' diverse meanings of,

103–4; American vs. French
concept of, 101; female icons
of, 7, 11–12, 13, 68, 101–2;
numerous French statues of,
57; schoolchildren's essays on,
185; as universal ideal, 193
Liberty Bell, 125, 157
"Liberty Enlightening the
World" (Bartholdi original
title), 6, 13, 39, 46, 66, 68, 76
"Liberty Enlightening the
World" (poem), 91
Liberty Guiding the People (Delacroix), 11, *12*, 101–2
Liberty Island (formerly Bedloe's
Island), 1–2, 6, 139, 193,
197–98; development of,
129–30, 131; ferry approach
to, 5; filmmakers and, 154–55,
156; Liberty Weekend and,
185, 186; lighting pits on,
180; naming of, 132; security
closure of, 158. *See also* Statue
of Liberty
Liberty Loans, 144–45, *146*,
149
Liberty Mutual Insurance
Company, 188
Liberty State Park (N.J.), 5–6
Liberty Weekend (1986), 74,
126, 131, 160, 175, 181–93;
commercial products and,
170–71; events of, 182–87;
exhibition catalogue for, 103;
financing of, 171; tourists and,
181–82, 185–86

Libeskind, Daniel, 192–93
Life (magazine), 81–82, 150–51
Lincoln, Abraham, 9, 10–11, 13
Lincoln, Mary Todd, 10–11
Lincoln Center (N.Y.C.), 116
Lincoln Memorial, 30
Lindsay, Mela Neisner, 115
Longfellow, Henry Wadsworth, 36
lottery, French, 56
Louvre, 46, 47
Lowell, James Russell, 119, 120
lynching, 99, 100

Mac-Mahon, Patrice de, 38, 39
Madison Square (N.Y.C.), 50, 78, 95
Mad magazine, *164*, 165
Manet, Edouard: *Déjeuner sur l'herbe*, 161
Marianne (French icon), 11, 101–2
Marti, José, 27
Marx, Karl, 25
Masonic symbolism, 28, 91
Mauss, Marcel, 74; *Essay on the Gift*, 74
McAdam, David, 185
McCormick Harvester Company, 96
McCullough, Colleen, 182
McDonald's (fast-food chain), 143, *144*
Medal of Liberty, U.S., 183
"melting pot" ideology, 116–17, 133–34; rejection of, 135

Mexican immigrants, 136, 191–92
Mexico, 10
Michel, André, 68
Michelangelo: *David*, 17
Millaud, Moses, 85
Miss Liberty (musical), 149
Moffitt, David, 186
Monduit, Honoré, 62
Mormons, 36
mother imagery, 16, 102, 124, 143
Mount Rushmore, 153, 171
Murrow, Edward R., 133

Napoleon I, 17, 27, 68
Napoleon III, 8–10, 11, 24, 37, 42–43, 51, 63
National Park Service, 129–37, 179, 180, 185, 186, 197; restoration process and, 166, 167; security measures of, 1–2, 158, 194–95
Nazi Germany, 124, 130–31, 150
neoclassicism, 3, 4, 6, 27, 28, 33, 68
"New Colossus, The" (Lazarus), 16–17, 151; entrance to Statue of Liberty and, 117, 119, 120; as fund-raising donation, 79–80, 119; "huddled masses" imagery and, 7, 104, 124, 149; Liberty's symbolism and, 123, 124
New Deal, 123–24, 126, 128–30, 149

New Jersey, 5–6, 156, 186
New Republic (magazine), 160,
    161, *162*
Newsday (newspaper), 184, 186
new social history, 135, 136
newspapers. *See* press
New York City: apocalyptic
    films and, 155–56; Bartholdi
    Lafayette statue for, 48, 77;
    Liberty Weekend and, 181–93;
    politics and, 84, 96–98;
    resilience of, 193; skyline of,
    1–2, 196; Statue of Liberty as
    monument to, 189
New York Daily News, 137
New Yorker (magazine), 190–91
New York Harbor, 100, 154, 196;
    diorama of Liberty in, 51, 52;
    immigrants arriving in, *169*,
    191; Statue of Liberty's
    position in, 2, 3, 4, 5, 31, 33,
    57, 71, 77, 78, 83, 89, 102,
    150, 188–89, 192; strong
    winds of, 59, 60, 92, 175–76,
    196; view from Statue of
    Liberty of, 174
New York Herald, 77, 84, 85
New York Morning Journal, 95
New York Sun, 84
New York Times, 48, 75, 78,
    80–81, 107, 117, 131, 188–89
New York Tribune, 84
New York World, 6, 84–89, 127,
    128
New York World-Telegram, 131
Niagara Falls, 36

Niederwald (German monu-
    ment), 67–68
9/11 attacks. *See* September 11
Nixon, Richard, 137, 157
Nora, Pierre, 43
North by Northwest (film), 153
North Korea, 17

Obama, Barack, 164, 165
Olmsted, Frederic Law, 35
Oudiné, Eugène-Andrée: "Medal
    of the Republic," 13

Palais de l'Industrie, 50–51
Palin, Sarah, 165
Pall, Ellen, 190–91
Panama Canal, 94
Panama Canal Zone, 183
Parc Morceau, 62
Paris: Haussmann redevelop-
    ment of, 51, 66; Liberty's
    construction in, 57–69;
    Liberty's storage in, 80;
    Liberty's visibility in, 66, 69,
    176; Prussian siege of, 24, 25
Paris Commune, 25, 26, 32, 35,
    46; U.S. reaction to, 38–39, 76
Paris International Exposition
    (1867), 24
Paris International Exposition
    (1878), 52–53, 64
Paris International Exposition
    (1889), 58
Paris Opera House, 47, 63
Parsons, Albert and Lucy, 97
Pauli, Hertha, 73

pedestal, 71, 90–92; American
funding of, 69–70, 73, 75–81,
84–89, 91; anchoring onto, 60;
architectural challenges of,
69–72; commencement of
work on, 90; cornerstone of,
87, 91; dimensions of, 70, 71;
early drawing of, 44–45, *44;*
elevator in, 128, 179; granite-
veneered concrete and, 91–92,
128; inscription on, 89;
interior steps of, 195; proportions of, 72; repairs to,
130, 179. *See also* foundation
Pei, I. M., 183
penny press, 51; Liberty's
celebrity status in, 83; power
of, 89; Pulitzer's small-donors
campaign and, 6, 84–89
Perlman, Itzhak, 183
Petit, Pierre, 62–63
Petit Journal, Le (daily), 42–43,
85
Pharos of Alexandria, 71–72
Philadelphia, 34, 35, 40, 49, 50,
69, 88, 89; bid for Statue of
Liberty in, 77–78. *See also*
centennial of American
independence
Philadelphia Evening Bulletin, 137
Philadelphia Press, 34, 77
Pitkin, Thomas M., 134
Planet of the Apes (film), 153–54,
155
Platt, Boss (Thomas C.), 110,
111

Plessy v. Ferguson (1896), 100
Polish immigrants, 122, 133,
136
political cartoons, 108–11, *112,*
120–21, 160–61, 163–65, 188;
common Liberty depictions in,
165
popular culture, 140–65
populism, 76, 82–83, 85, 87
postage stamps, U.S., 132, 140,
190
Powell, Adam Clayton, 135, 136
presidential election of 1876, 86
presidential election of 1884, 86,
87, 137
presidential election of 1988,
187, 188
press, 6, 50, 64–65, 77–78,
80–89, 91; French fund-raising
and, 41, 42–47, 52, 64, 83;
immigration opposition and,
108–13; Statue of Liberty
publicity and, 34, 50. *See also*
penny press; *specific publications*
Progressive era, 126, 127–29
Protean Wisdom (website),
164–65
Protestantism, 79, 106
Prussia. *See* Germany
Public Health Service, 113–14
Public Works Administration,
130
Puck (magazine), 98, 110, *111,*
142; Puerto Rican nationalists,
157
Puerto Ricans, 134

Pulitzer, Joseph, 76, 80, 82, 84–89, 127, 131, 168; "Appeal to Patriotism" campaign of, 6, 87–88; background of, 84–85

Qaeda, Al, 2, 158, 190
Quebec separatists, 157
Quick (French fast-food chain), 143
Quotidien, Le (newspaper), 68–69

Radical Republicans, 28
railway bridges, 58–59
Rapp, Jean, 18–19
Reagan, Nancy, 185
Reagan, Ronald, 167, 181, 182, 183, 187–88
Reconstruction era, 28, 99
Red Scare, 120, 122
Regan, Donald, 188
Rémusat, Charles de, 8
Rémusat, Paul de, 40
repoussé metalwork, 172
Republican Party, 38, 84–86, 96, 110, 187
restoration (1986), 94, 103, 126, 166–80, 187, 196; asbestos removal and, 178; French experts' diagnoses and, 166–67, 171; interior and, 178–80; key issues of, 171–72; power-washing and, 177; preservationists vs. modern technology and, 174–75, 177, 178, 180; sale of souvenir scrap metal from, 171, 178; scaffold-ing and, 175–76; small-donor fund-raising for, 168–70; structural problems and, 173–75
Rice, Condoleezza, 165
Robbins, Jerome, 149
Rochambeau, marquis de, 42
Roebling, John A., 35
Roosevelt, Franklin D., 123–24, 126, 129
Roosevelt, Theodore, 84, 116, 127
Roosevelt Memorial, 30
Root and Tinker print, 141
Russian immigrants, 105, 118, 119, 122, 168–69

Sabin, Albert, 183
Saboteur (film), 151–53, 156, 172
St. Louis Post-Dispatch, 84
San Francisco, 36–37, 78
San Francisco Daily, 78
Savorgnan de Brazza, Pierre, 51
Scheffer, Ary, 21
Schwanthaler, Ludwig: *Bavaria*, 17, *19*
science fiction, 155–56, 158–59
Scots-Irish immigrants, 105–6
Seagram's, 170
Secrétan, Pierre-Eugène, 45
segregation, 100, 104
September 11 (2001), 4, 156; Freedom Tower memorial, 192–93; Statue of Liberty security and, 1–2, 5, 158, 194
sexuality, 101–2, 160–63

Shea, John Gilmory, 79
Sherwood, Robert E., 149
Simonin, Louis-Laurent, 24
Singer sewing machines, 142–43
skyscrapers, 60
slavery: Liberty's broken chains
    of, 28. *See also* abolitionism
Smirnoff, Yakov, 186
Sopranos, The (TV series), 5–6
souvenirs, 54–56, 79, 95; gift
    shop and, 197; Liberty
    Weekend and, 186, 188;
    Philadelphia centennial and,
    49–50, 140; restoration scrap
    metal as, 171, 178
Spanish-speaking immigrants,
    122, 134, 183–84, 191–92
Spielberg, Steven, 159
Spitzer, Eliot, 163
Splash (film), 154–55
Statue of Liberty: American early
    resistance to, 69, 73–74, 79,
    80–81; American identity
    of, 36, 98–101, 149–53; as
    America's primary icon, 3, 77,
    125, 130, 131, 132, 187, 192;
    androgyny of, 28; anthropo-
    morphism of, 55, 83–84;
    appearance of, 5, 6, 7, 176–77;
    artistic merit of, 3, 4, 80–81;
    ascent to top of, 58, 179–80,
    194, 195–96; as beacon, 180;
    building of (*see* construction);
    centennial of (*see* Liberty
    Weekend); color of, 5, 7,
    176–77; commercialization

of, 54–55, 142–65, 170, 188;
    cornerstone contents of, 91;
    critics of, 79, 91; dignity
    retention of, 188–89; as
    engineering/technological
    masterpiece, 57–72; essential
    qualities of, 3–4; fiftieth
    anniversary celebration of,
    123–24; film and video use of,
    151–56, 158–60; financial cost
    of, 40; as Franco-American
    united effort, 3, 6, 10; French
    genesis of, 8–29, 34–35, 73,
    74, 75, 80–83 (*see also* Bar-
    tholdi, Frédéric Auguste); as
    gift from France, 2, 10, 32, 43,
    73, 79, 132, 133, 185; immi-
    grants' first sight of, 114–15,
    122, 168–69 (*see also* immi-
    gration); interior staircases of,
    58, 174, 194, 195, 196–97;
    Lazarus poem and, 7, 16–17,
    79, 104, 117, 119, 120, 124,
    149; lighting of, 128, 180,
    181, 182, 187; literary use of,
    116–17, 119–20; malleable
    meanings of, 3, 4, 12, 76–77,
    83, 97–98, 103–25, 129,
    139, 145–49, 153–56, 188;
    meaning/symbolism of, 2, 3,
    5, 7, 18, 23, 28, 29, 41, 45–46,
    68, 76–77, 80, 94, 98, 124–25,
    139, 140, 166–67, 171, 174,
    189, 191, 192; mother imagery
    of, 16, 102, 124; national
    monument status of, 128,

129–30, 139, 174; negative
connotations of, 104, 123;
physical deterioration of,
126–29, 131, 166, 173–74, 177
(*see also* restoration); physical
threats to, 156–58; political
cartoon images of, 108–11,
120–21, 160–61, 163–65;
popularity of, 83–84, 131–32;
replicas of, 54–55, 68, 79,
115–16, 189–90; sculptural
lineage of, 17–22, 27; security
measures for, 1–2, 5, 153,
158, 193, 194–95; site of (*see*
Liberty Island); size of, 5;
theater portrayals of, 116–17,
145–49; unveiling of (1886),
73, 94–98, 101, 103; view
from, 5, 174, 179–80, 195–96;
visibility of, 2, 31, 73; visitors'
center for, 130 (*see also* tourists); World War II and,
130–31. *See also* arm; crown;
foundation; head; pedestal;
torch
Statue of Liberty–Ellis Island
Centennial Commission
(public), 167–68
Statue of Liberty–Ellis Island
Commission, 188
Statue of Liberty–Ellis Island
Foundation (private), 167–68
Steiner, Edward, 115
Stone, Charles P., 70, 90, 91
strikes (1877–80s), 39, 96–97, 98,
104, 107

Suez Canal, 21
suffrage, 38, 101, 104
Sumner, Charles, 34
Superman IV (film), 158
Supreme Court, U.S., 99, 100
Swank Hayden Connell (archi-
tects), 167

tablet of laws (Statue of Liberty),
28, 44, *63*, 196
Talbott, Hudson: *Luncheon on the
Grass*, 161–62, *163*
Tammany Hall, 84
television, 160, 182, 186
terra cotta models, 54–55, 79
terrorism: Statue of Liberty and,
1–2, 153, 158. *See also* September 11
Terror of 1793–94 (France), 4,
12, 13
Thiers, Adolphe, 26
Tiananmen Square protest
(1989), 190–91
Tilden, Samuel J., 86
Tocqueville, Alexis de, 35;
Democracy in America, 8
Tocqueville, Hippolyte de, 8,
40, 41
torch, 7, 22, 28, 44, 102, 172,
192, 196; as advertising image,
141–42; damage/off-limits to
visitors of, 156; display of,
47–50, 52, 140; flame recre-
ation and, 171–72; lighting
process for, 93, 128, 180;
replica of, 116; restoration

torch (continued)
of, 171–72, 178; structural
engineering of, 60, 175;
visitors' viewing platform in,
60
tourists, 5, 50, 56, 126, 129–30,
193, 194–98; American
Museum of Immigration and,
137; interior accessibility and,
179–80; internationality of,
2, 7, 197; Liberty Weekend
and, 181–83, 185–86; numbers
of, 1–2, 131, 186; postwar
increase in, 131, 140
Trachtenberg, Marvin, 60
Tresca, Carlo, 122
triumphal arches, 17
Trump, Donald, 160–61
Tumulty, T. James, 138
Turgenev, Ivan, 117
Turner, Henry McNeil, 99
Twain, Mark, 80–81

Uncle Sam, 125
undocumented immigrants, 192,
197
Union League Club, 34–35, 40,
69–70, 96
Union Square (N.Y.C.): Bartholdi Lafayette statue in, 48,
77
universities, 135, 136
University of Minnesota, 136
University of Pennsylvania,
187

Vanderbilt, Cornelius, 75–76
Vanderbilt, William K., 89
Vecoli, Rudolph J., 136
Verne, James: *Around the World
in Eighty Days*, 85
video games, 159–60, 188
Vietnam Veterans Against the
War, 157
Vietnam War, 139
Village Voice (newspaper), 164
Viollet-le-Duc, Eugène, 63
V Magazine, 162–63

Walker, Tommy, 185
Walkley, A. B., 117
Wallace, David, 136–37
Walters, Barbara, 182
Wang, An, 183
War Department, U.S., 128
Wards Island, 119
Washburne, Elihu, 47
Washington, George, 41, 91
Washington Monument, 30,
157
Washington Post, 187
Weill, Kurt: *Johnny Johnson*,
145–49, 159
Weiss, Arnold, 114
Whitman, Walt, 117
Wiesel, Elie, 183
Wilson, Woodrow, 128
Windom, William, 107–8, 109,
110
Wolper, David, 182, 183, 184,
185, 186

Woman Suffrage Association,
101
women: advertising images of,
143; as allegorical "liberty," 7,
11–12, 13, 68, 101–2; Liberty's
centennial and, 183; Liberty's
unveiling ceremony and, 101;
as mother figure, 16, 102, 124,
143; sexuality imagery and,
160–64
women's lib movement, *164*, 165
women's rights, 35, 101
women's suffrage, 101, 104
Works Progress Administration,
130

World Trade Center site,
192–93
World War I, 113, 120, 122,
144–45, *146*, 149, 156, 196
World War II, 124, 130–31,
138, 145, *147*, 149–53

xenophobia, 3, 108–11, *112*,
120–21, 125

Young, Brigham, 36

Zangwill, Israel, 116–17, 120;
The Melting Pot, 116–17
Zannini, Alexandre, 24